T0312795

ALTA VIA 2 – TREKKING IN THE DOLOMITES

ALTA VIA 2 – TREKKING IN THE DOLOMITES

INCLUDES 1:25,000 MAP BOOKLET.
WITH ALTE VIE 3–6 IN OUTLINE

by Gillian Price

JUNIPER HOUSE, MURLEY MOSS,
OXENHOLME ROAD, KENDAL, CUMBRIA LA9 7RL
www.cicerone.co.uk

© Gillian Price 2022
Fifth edition 2022
ISBN: 978 1 78631 097 2
Reprinted 2024 (with updates)
Fourth edition 2016
Third edition 2011
Second edition 2005
First edition 1990

Printed in China on responsibly sourced paper on behalf of Latitude Press Ltd
A catalogue record for this book is available from the British Library.
All photographs are by the author unless otherwise stated.

Route mapping by Lovell Johns www.lovelljohns.com
Contains OpenStreetMap.org data © OpenStreetMap
contributors, CC-BY-SA. NASA relief data courtesy of ESRI

Mapping in map booklet © KOMPASSKarten GmbH
cartography 2022 (licence number: 41-0921-LIV).
Copying and reproduction prohibited

Acknowledgements

Thanks to Georgia Laval for her patient editing, Natalie, Clare and the Cicerone team for a great job, Nick for the route diagrams, Stefano Zannini and CAI Feltre for their work on the concluding stages of the AV2, and all the walkers who wrote in with feedback and comments on previous editions.

For the one-and-only Nick. But he has to share with dear departed Danilo and Piero, generous souls who actively encouraged me to discover these magical mountains in my infant alpine years.

Front cover: A steep ascent over scree leads to Forcella della Roa (AV2, Stage 3)

CONTENTS

Updates to this Guide

While every effort is made by our authors to ensure the accuracy of guidebooks as they go to print, changes can occur during the lifetime of an edition. This guidebook was researched and written during the COVID-19 pandemic. While we are not aware of any significant changes to routes or facilities at the time of printing, it is likely that the current situation will give rise to more changes than would usually be expected. Any updates that we know of for this guide will be on the Cicerone website (www.cicerone.co.uk/1097/updates), so please check before planning your trip. We also advise that you check information about such things as transport, accommodation and shops locally. Even rights of way can be altered over time.

We are always grateful for information about any discrepancies between a guidebook and the facts on the ground, sent by email to updates@cicerone.co.uk or by post to Cicerone, Juniper House, Murley Moss, Oxenholme Road, Kendal, LA9 7RL.

Register your book: to sign up to receive free updates, special offers and GPX files where available, register your book at www.cicerone.co.uk.

Legend for route overview maps

═══════	sealed road	⬆	accommodation & meals
·····O·····	railway	⬆	bivouac hut
────────	walk route	🌡	gondola lift
··········	walk variant	🚡	cable-car
	crest, mountain peak	🪑	chair lift
	watercourse	🚌	bus
⤳	pass		

Symbols used on route maps

~~	route
- - -	alternative route
(S)	start point
(F)	finish point
>	route direction
	woodland
	urban areas
•	other feature
▬■▬	railway/station
(cable car)	cable car
(gondola lift)	gondola lift
(chair lift)	chair lift
▲	peak
■	building
⬆	mountain hut
⬘	bivouac hut
◇	other accommodation
(food)	food
(ATM)	ATM
(bus)	bus stop/station
P	parking
†	cross
▲	monument
⌣	pass
(i)	tourist information

Relief
in metres

3600–3800	
3400–3600	
3200–3400	
3000–3200	
2800–3000	
2600–2800	
2400–2600	
2200–2400	
2000–2200	
1800–2000	
1600–1800	
1400–1600	
1200–1400	
1000–1200	
800–1000	
600–800	
400–600	
200–400	
0–200	

SCALE: 1:75,000

0 kms   0.5   1
0 miles   0.5

Contour lines are
drawn at 25m intervals
and highlighted at
100m intervals.

GPX files for all routes can be downloaded free at www.cicerone.co.uk/1097/GPX.

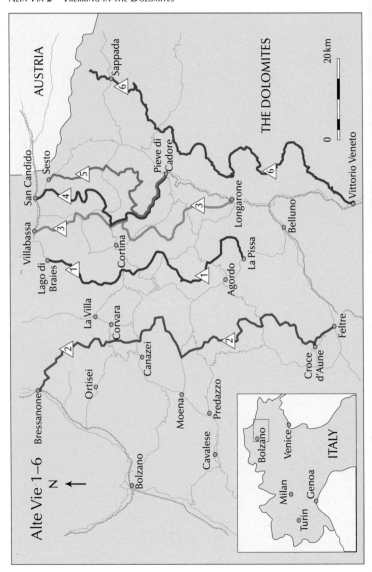

The magnificent Croda Rossa features in AV3

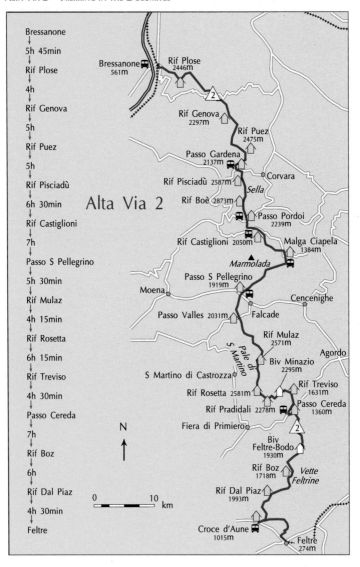

Bressanone
↓ 5h 45min
Rif Plose
↓ 4h
Rif Genova
↓ 5h
Rif Puez
↓ 5h
Rif Pisciadù
↓ 6h 30min
Rif Castiglioni
↓ 7h
Passo S Pellegrino
↓ 5h 30min
Rif Mulaz
↓ 4h 15min
Rif Rosetta
↓ 6h 15min
Rif Treviso
↓ 4h 30min
Passo Cereda
↓ 7h
Rif Boz
↓ 6h
Rif Dal Piaz
↓ 4h 30min
Feltre

Alta Via 2

ROUTE SUMMARY TABLE – ALTA VIA 2

Stage	From	To	Time	Distance	Ascent/Descent	Grade	Page
1	Bressanone	Rifugio Plose	5hr 45min	12km	1910m/20m	2	41
2	Rifugio Plose	Rifugio Genova	4hr	13.5km	680m/530m	2	45
3	Rifugio Genova	Rifugio Puez	5hr	12km	840m/660m	2–3	51
4	Rifugio Puez	Rifugio Pisciadù	5hr	10km	900m/800m	3	55
5	Rifugio Pisciadù	Rifugio Castiglioni	6hr 30min	16km	690m/1230m	3	60
6	Rifugio Castiglioni	Passo San Pellegrino	7hr	22km	1110m/1240m	2	67
7	Passo San Pellegrino	Rifugio Mulaz	5hr 30min	13km	1040m/380m	3	74
8	Rifugio Mulaz	Rifugio Rosetta	4hr 15min	7.5km	750m/740m	3+	80
9	Rifugio Rosetta	Rifugio Treviso	6hr 15min	13km	790m/1740m	3	86
10	Rifugio Treviso	Passo Cereda	4hr 30min	8.5km	750m/1010m	2–3	93
11	Passo Cereda	Rifugio Boz	7hr	13.5km	1250m/900m	3	97
12	Rifugio Boz	Rifugio Dal Piaz	6hr	14km	940m/670m	3	102
13	Rifugio Dal Piaz	Feltre	4hr 30min	19km	negligible/1820m	2	107
Total			**71hr 15min**	**174km**	**11,650m/11,740m**		

Mountain safety

Every mountain walk has its dangers, and those described in this guidebook are no exception. All who walk or climb in the mountains should recognise this and take responsibility for themselves and their companions along the way. The author and publisher have made every effort to ensure that the information contained in this guide was correct when it went to press, but, except for any liability that cannot be excluded by law, they cannot accept responsibility for any loss, injury or inconvenience sustained by any person using this book.

International distress signal *(emergency only)*
Six blasts on a whistle (and flashes with a torch after dark) spaced evenly for one minute, followed by a minute's pause. Repeat until an answer is received. The response is three signals per minute followed by a minute's pause.

Helicopter rescue
The following signals are used to communicate with a helicopter:

 Help needed:
raise both arms
above head to
form a 'Y'

 Help not needed:
raise one arm
above head, extend
other arm downward

Emergency telephone numbers
General emergency tel 112
Soccorso alpino (mountain rescue) tel 118

Weather reports
Südtirol https://weather.provinz.bz.it
Trentino www.meteotrentino.it
Veneto www.arpa.veneto.it

Mountain rescue can be very expensive – be adequately insured.

PREFACE TO THIS EDITION

This brand new edition focuses on the spectacular Alta Via 2 across my favourite mountains, the Dolomites. Nicola and I discovered the trek bit by bit, beginning for some long-forgotten reason at the southern end, traversing the rugged Vette Feltrine. Vast bodies of swirling fog were constant companions blotting out views – and the sense of exposure (luckily, as I found out later). Next came the magical Pale di San Martino and the awesome Sella massif with thrilling ibex sightings. Then we decided to put the whole thing together and walk it properly, north to south – once, twice, lost count… Simply magnificent. And with the recent extension down to Feltre, it now means that you walk out of Bressanone railway station at the trek start and finish at Feltre railway station at the end.

This guidebook provides up-to-date details that will help make this stunning trek easy for visitors to handle and organise, and it is supplemented with new mapping in a separate booklet.

UNESCO added the Dolomites to its World Heritage list in 2009 and visitor numbers have soared. Now it is even more important to emphasise responsible management helped by environment-conscious walkers to ensure this paradise can be enjoyed by future generations.

Gillian Price, Venice

Climbing away from Pian dei Cantoni (AV2, Stage 8)

INTRODUCTION

Passo Gardena and the Sella come into view on Stage 4 of AV2

THE DOLOMITES

Awesome, dramatic, and downright beautiful, the Dolomite mountains account for the northeastern corner of Italy close to its border with Austria. Delicately pale peaks and sculpted rock spires soar to dizzy heights, and breathtaking sheer walls tower over high-altitude lunar-like plateaux and plunging scree valleys.

These UNESCO World Heritage mountains are a wonderland for summer walkers. An excellent web of marked pathways snake over mountain and across vale, supported by a network of brilliantly located and hospitable *rifugi* mountain huts that welcome walkers, feed them royally and put them up overnight. Nature lovers will be delighted by settings reminiscent of *The Sound of Music*, with vast expanses of sweet alpine meadows transformed into seas of multicoloured wildflowers in the summer months. Magnificent dense evergreen and deciduous forests are widespread, as is fascinating wildlife. In all, an extraordinary array of landscapes.

Adventurous visitors can enjoy the magnificence day after day by embarking on a long-distance trek. Six established high-level walking trails traverse the Dolomites from top to bottom, north to south. Known singly as Alta Via (abbreviated as AV) 'high way', or *Höhenweg* in German, they maintain medium to high altitude and explore spectacular corners of the different groups. On any one *alta via*, walkers can expect to see up to 80% of all the Dolomites!

This guidebook focuses on describing AV2 in detail, along with summarised versions of AVs 3, 4, 5 and 6; AV1 on the other hand comes under a separate cover.

ALTA VIA 2

Alta Via 2 is the perfect first Dolomites trek for experienced walkers (or the perfect second trek after AV1). Dubbed the 'Alta Via delle Leggende', this challenging and memorable route links the baroque town of Bressanone in the northwest with Renaissance-style Feltre in the far south. It's 174km long and strays as high as 2907m. Well marked and straightforward to follow, it entails aided and exposed sections, although several can be detoured. Along the way AV2 visits the Plose massif, the jagged Puez-Odle and its vast plateau, the forbidding fortress-like Sella, the majestic Marmolada (the highest mountain in the Dolomites at 3342m), the spectacular Pale di San Martino and the rugged Alpi Feltrine group. (The handy PeakFinder app can help you put all the right names to the mountains you see.)

The trek has been divided into 13 day-stages for the purposes of this guide, fitting snugly into a two-week vacation. Shorter chunks are definitely feasible if you have less holiday time – see 'Shorter itineraries', below. Each stage concludes at an alpine *rifugio* with accommodation and meals, and there's occasionally a hotel choice too. This means you can travel light. Naturally, self-sufficient trekkers can camp out, enabling greater flexibility, although restrictions do apply – see 'Accommodation' below. There is absolutely no reason why the stages cannot be lengthened or shortened; everyone walks at a different pace and there's a host of intermediate stopover accommodation along the way.

ALTA VIA 1

Renowned and justifiably popular, AV1 is a suitable beginner's trek in the Dolomites, straightforward yet extremely rewarding. Connecting beautiful Lago di Braies with Belluno, it is spread over 11 days and almost 120km, with a high point of 2752m. It visits the Fanes area, the Lagazuoi and Cortina mountains with the Cinque Torri and Pelmo, before moving on to the magnificent Civetta, Moiazza and the Dolomiti Bellunesi. See the separate Cicerone guidebook *Alta Via 1 – Trekking in the Dolomites*.

Exit routes are also given throughout, along with transport info – essential for emergencies, bad weather or a change of plan. They also double as handy entry routes if you prefer to customise the trek to fit in with personal holiday dictates.

ALTE VIE 3–6

The four other AVs – 3, 4, 5 and 6 – are more demanding and solitary. In this guide they are presented in summary, giving the flavour and difficulty of each; diagram route maps show facilities and transport. They make their way across a combination of well-trodden and wilder mountain chains and on the whole see fewer walkers. By and large, climbing experience is essential as stretches of

via ferrata are the flavour of the day, and trekkers need to be prepared to carry their own food, sleeping and cooking gear, as several nights are spent in unmanned bivouac huts as well as *rifugi*. Notwithstanding, the average walker will find straightforward village-to-village and hut-to-hut chunks are easily detached. A host of variants exist, not all covered in this guide.

Although the routes are described north–south here, there is no reason they cannot be followed in the opposite direction – recalculate times in relation to ascent/descent.

In the Dolomites in general the extensive web of marked pathways, refuges and capillary public transport means that anyone can concoct their own itinerary. A host of suggestions

The Cristallo across from Rifugio Vallandro (AV3)

for multi-day treks can be found in the Cicerone guide *Walking in the Dolomites*, as well as single-day routes in *Shorter Walks in the Dolomites*.

GEOLOGY

A little geology goes a long way in understanding the Dolomites. The Monti Pallidi or 'Pale Mounts' as they were originally called, were rechristened in honour of a French mineralogist marquis with the unforgettable name Déodat Guy Sylvain Tancrède Gratet de Dolomieu. Intrigued as to why they differed so dramatically from other ranges, after a 1789 visit he discovered the main rock as calcium magnesium carbonate (later called dolomite in his honour), which shares the show with limestone, namely calcium carbonate.

The mountains date back some 230 million years to when the region was covered by a shallow tropical sea. Remains of sea creatures and much else accumulated bit by bit on its floor. These compressed and hardened over time into sedimentary rock incorporating fossilised shells, coral, ripple marks and even tracks left by dinosaurs. Much later, around 65 million years ago, land-moving tectonic events thrust the rock dramatically upwards, as the Alps were created. Over time ice ages and glaciers shaped the mountains, and they are subject to ongoing erosion by wind and rain – the vast scree flows are a good example.

According to legend, the rock surface of the Dolomites is covered in fine white gossamer woven from moon rays, to help acclimatise a princess bride pining for the lunar landscapes of her homeland. At sundown these pale rock faces assume gorgeous hues of orangey-pink, a spectacular phenomenon known as *enrosadira*.

LANGUAGES AND PLACE NAMES

In 1919, in the aftermath of the World War 1 hostilities between the crumbling Austro-Hungarian Empire and the fledgling Republic of Italy, the whole of the Dolomites became Italian, forming a fascinating cultural and linguistic mosaic. During the ensuing Fascist period, every single place name – mountains included – was translated into Italian, although both Italian and German are commonly used in the region now.

Nowadays the Südtirol/Alto Adige region, with its capital Bozen/Bolzano, is dominated by German-language speakers – 70% of the population, though most people are bilingual. The inhabitants of the adjoining Trentino region, centred on the splendid city of Trento, are all Italian speakers. Likewise those in the remaining southeastern chunk of the Dolomites, which comes under the Veneto region, long administered from Venice. However, local dialect place names abound.

An old wartime track snakes its way downhill on AV2, Stage 13

Ancient tongues are still heard. The Rhaeto-Romanic language known as Ladin (predating the Latin brought by the Romans) has survived in good shape and is the declared mother tongue of just over 4% of the inhabitants of the Dolomites. Lastly there's an intriguing linguistic pocket in the easternmost town of Sappada where Plodarisch, an old Bavarian–Tyrolean dialect, is still spoken.

Maps and signposts use Italian, German and Ladin versions of place names – a little confusing for visitors. An obvious example is the term *rifugio*, *Hütte* in German, transformed into *Ücia* or *Ütia* in Ladin. Be prepared for minor discrepancies between maps and signposts as well as the map booklet, as changes are ongoing. For the purposes of this guidebook, to keep things simple and avoid crowding the text, Italian is mostly given

precedence. See Appendix B for an Italian–English glossary containing terms that might be useful on the trail.

PLANTS AND FLOWERS

The Dolomites boast 1400 species of glorious flowering plants – around a fifth of Italy's total. Throughout the summer months it's impossible not to be impressed by the amazing spreads of blooms in the most unlikely and inhospitable spots. Heading the list in popularity is the edelweiss, its creamy felty petals forming a star. In dramatic colour contrast are the deep-blue trumpet gentians that burst through the grass, demanding admiration. In lush meadows, gorgeous orange lilies and the wine-red martagon variety vie with each other for brilliance. Light larch woodland and slopes are colonised by spreads of alpenrose, a type

(Clockwise from top L) Moretti's bellflower; Edelweiss; Rhaetian poppies; orange lily

of rhododendron that has masses of pretty red-pink flowers. Its neighbours are low bushes of bilberries, laden with tiny sweet fruit in late summer.

One of the earliest blooms to appear is the Alpine snowbell – its fragile fringed blue-lilac bells even sprout in snow patches thanks to an 'anti-freeze' carbohydrate. Never far away are delicate pasque flowers in white or yellow.

Shaded clearings are the place to look for the unusual lady's-slipper orchid, recognisable by a swollen yellow lip crowned by maroon petals, while pyramidal purple or cone-shaped black vanilla orchids are common on rich pasture. Perfumed fluttery Rhaetian poppies brighten bleached scree slopes with patches of yellow and orange, companions to clumps of pink thrift or round-leaved pennycress, which is honey-scented. Another rock coloniser is saxifrage, literally 'rock breaker', so called for its deep-reaching roots.

A rare treat is devil's claw, which specialises in hanging off vertical rock faces. A member of the rampion family, it sports a segmented pointy lilac flower with curly stigma. Another precious bloom is the king of the Alps, a striking cushion of pretty blue, almost a dwarf version of the forget-me-not. Moretti's bellflower with rounded deep-blue petals nestles in high crevices in the southern Dolomites. Dry sun-scorched terrain is preferred by curious houseleeks, which bear an uncanny resemblance to miniature triffids.

As far as trees go, over 1000m is the realm of conifers such as silver fir along with 'high achievers' arolla pine and larch, which can reach 2600m altitudes. A great coloniser and anchor on scree is the dwarf mountain pine, whose springy branches invade paths. One remarkable 'bonsai' tree is the net-leaved willow, whose closely packed root system creeps over rock surfaces.

WILDLIFE

It seems a miracle that wild animals still call the European Alps home. As if the harsh environment and climate weren't enough, they also have to deal with ongoing threats from mankind in the shape of roads, expanding ski pistes and resorts; selective hunting is also allowed in some valleys, albeit under strict controls. The good news is that much of the Dolomites comes under the protection of nature parks: Dolomiti di Sesto, Sciliar, Fanes-Senes-Braies, Dolomiti d'Ampezzo, Puez-Odle, Pale di San Martino and Dolomiti Bellunesi – and AV2 traverses the last three.

The easiest animals to see when you're out walking are alpine marmots. These adorable furry creatures look a bit like beavers (without the flat tail) and live in extensive underground colonies. Wary of foxes and golden eagles who can carry off their young, they always have a sentry posted – an older animal who stands rod-straight and emits heart-stopping warning whistles to summon the tribe back home. Alpine marmots hibernate from October to April, waking once a month to urinate. Now protected in Italy, they were once hunted throughout the Alps for their skins and fat, and paraded in street fairs.

Higher up, impossibly steep rock faces and scree slopes are the ideal terrain for shy, fleet-hoofed chamois – slender mountain goats with short crochet-hook horns and fawn coats. Herds of females with their young graze on pasture flats, separate from old itinerant males whose sharp poignant whistle gives them away in the bushes. Chamois head down into

Alpine marmots are easy to spot; chamois are experts on rock faces

valleys when the snow starts falling, sharing the forest habitat with graceful Bambi-like roe deer and the rarer large red species.

Ibex are an exciting sight. These stocky animals sport impressively thick grooved horns that curve backwards, up to a metre long on males, who can weigh 100kg; the females less on both counts. During the summer, young males spend time in mock battle, clashing their horns in preparation for the December mating season when it is anything but pretend, as the females are only on heat for 24 hours. Ibex were successfully reintroduced to the Dolomites in the 1970s from the single surviving alpine group in the Valle d'Aosta. Large herds are often encountered in the eastern Dolomites.

Brown bears once roamed freely, as testified by place names such as Col dell'Orso (bear's col) and Buco dell'Orso (bear's hole). They were hunted to near extinction in the 1800s but a tiny nucleus hung on in the western Dolomites. Now protected, their numbers have been boosted by arrivals from Slovenia; the population is currently estimated at 50–60. Sightings and fleeting encounters are becoming more common in the Trentino region, where they are an increasing nuisance to both shepherds and beekeepers.

The European wolf, on the other hand, has required no help at all. Originating from a group in the central Apennines, elegant grey wolves have slowly but surely come north and spread stealthily across the Italian Alps, successfully establishing packs and sometimes attacking livestock when wild prey is unavailable. In the extremely unlikely event that you see either of these animals, use your common sense and keep your distance. Under no circumstances should they be approached.

Birdwatchers will enjoy the small, delightful songsters in woods, and sizeable birds of prey such as kites, buzzards and golden eagles above the tree line. One special treat is the lammergeier or bearded vulture, back in the Alps after centuries of persecution. Easy to recognise for its orange neck ruff and impressive 3m wingspan, the bird glides low in search of an abandoned carcass: it extracts bones to drop on rocks, breaking them open to eat.

A delight to watch is the showy high-altitude wallcreeper, a bit like a woodpecker. Fluttering like a butterfly over extraordinarily sheer rock faces in its hunt for insects, it flashes its black plumage with red panels and white dots, attracting attention with its shrill piping call.

Probably the most memorable bird in the Dolomites is the cheeky scavenging alpine chough, a type of crow with a bright yellow-orange beak. Noisy flocks of these ubiquitous and gregarious birds perform acrobatics at high altitudes. Attracted by the slightest rustle of a food wrapper, they appear out of nowhere, hovering optimistically in the sure knowledge that all walkers stop at cols for a snack, leaving behind inevitable crumbs (and hopefully nothing else).

Now that terrible dragons have been banished from the Alps, the only other potentially dangerous encounters concern snakes and ticks. Hot weather and open terrain could mean an encounter with an adder or viper (*vipera* in Italian). Tawny brown with a diamond-shaped head and distinctive zigzag markings along its back, they grow up to 70cm. Vipers are venomous but only attack under threat, so if you meet one – on a path where it is sunning itself and may be sluggish – step back and give it time to slither away to safety. In the unlikely event of

BACKGROUND READING

Plenty of inspirational travel accounts from the mid 1800s and early 1900s are available in libraries and on the web and make for delicious reading. John Murray's *Handbook for Travellers in Southern Germany* with its enthralling descriptions of the Dolomites was a pioneering work from 1840. Later came the groundbreaking travel log *The Dolomite Mountains: Excursions through Tyrol, Carinthia, Carniola, and Friuli* by Josiah Gilbert and GC Churchill (1864). One of the best reads is Amelia Edwards' 1873 *Untrodden Peaks and Unfrequented Valleys: A Midsummer Ramble in the Dolomites*. Hard on its heels in 1875 came renowned mountaineer DW Freshfield's *Italian Alps: Sketches in the Mountains of Ticino, Lombardy, the Trentino, and Venetia*, which is especially poetic. Of great interest for flower hunters is the historic *The Dolomites* by Reginald Farrer (1913) as well as the modern-day Cicerone pocket guide *Alpine Flowers*, a valuable aid.

a bite (very rarely fatal), stay put and seek help immediately.

As regards the tick – *zecca* in Italian – some may carry Lyme disease or TBE (tick-borne encephalitis), life-threatening for humans. Warnings apply for the southern Dolomites, especially wooded areas with thick undergrowth where ticks can latch onto you. Precautions include wearing long trousers and spraying boots, clothing and hat (but not skin!) with an insect repellent containing permethrin. Inspect yourself carefully after a walk for suspect black spots or itching. Remove any ticks very carefully using tweezers – be sure to get the head out – and disinfect the skin. Consult a doctor if you are concerned or experience any symptoms. For more information see www.lymeneteurope.org.

HOW TO GET THERE

The Dolomites are located in the northeast of Italy, not far from the border with Austria. Alta Via 2 begins on their northwestern edge at the town of Bressanone, known as Brixen in German. It has a railway station.

By train

A logical approach from northern Europe and the UK is by rail – a leisurely and less polluting option than flying. From London, one possible route is by Eurostar to Paris (www.eurostar.com) then TGV to Munich (www.sncf.com). Change here (www.

bahn.com) for Innsbruck then the Brenner Pass before alighting at Bressanone in Italy.

By plane to Venice, then train

Many walkers will be flying in to Venice's Marco Polo airport (www.veniceairport.com). There, a local bus can be taken to Mestre railway station for the train via Verona to Bressanone (www.trenitalia.com).

By plane to Treviso, then train

Should your flight be scheduled into Treviso (www.trevisoairport.it), catch the local bus to Treviso railway station for the train (www.trenitalia.com) via Verona to Bressanone.

By plane to Verona, then train

Verona's Valerio Catullo aiport (www.aeroportoverona.it) has a shuttle bus to Verona Porta Nuova railway station where you can pick up a train north to Bressanone.

By train from Venice

A further variant is the train directly from Venice (Venezia Santa Lucia) via Verona. In addition to Trenitalia, Austrian Rail has several direct runs (www.oebb.at).

Getting home

From the end of AV2 at Feltre, there are train services to Treviso and Venice as well as Trentino Trasporti buses to Trento for rail connections back to Bressanone if needed.

Tickets

For Italian trains, unless you have a digital ticket and/or booked seat – in which case your ticket will show a date and time – stamp your ticket in one of the machines on the platform before boarding. Failure to do so can result in a fine.

For buses, where possible, purchase tickets on websites or at ticket offices (often the local café) to save holding up the driver. There may be a small surcharge if you buy on board. Many of the transport companies listed in this guide now have an app where you can purchase tickets and check timetables.

WHEN TO GO

For walkers on the Alte Vie the season begins in mid to late June as the huts open. At this time some snow cover can still be expected on high cols and plateaus such as the Sella and Altipiano di San Martino, although naturally the situation varies year by year. July can be marvellous with long days and brilliant flowers. August spells more people and busier accommodation but more favourable path conditions. Generally speaking, Italian alpine summers mean sunshine and heat, relieved by storms that build up during the day. While short and sweet, they are often intense, bringing rain, thunder and lightning and occasionally hail or even snow, along with an abrupt drop in temperature.

September to October is the tail part of the Dolomites season and usually translates into crystal-clear skies – none of that summer humidity and haze – and quieter paths. The downside is the vegetation, as the intense alpine green will have faded, gradually replaced by yellows and pre-autumn shades. The chance of an odd storm and possibly a flurry or two of snow on high reaches are also on the cards. Lastly, you'll need to check that huts are still operating. Those in the northern Dolomites (the Südtirol region) tend to stay open longer (through to October) than those in the southern districts, which shut late September.

SHORTER ITINERARIES

It takes an average walker a total of 13 days to complete the AV2; however, if you have less time or walk faster, shorter chunks or combinations are feasible. Below are some suggestions. Note that all the start and finish points are served by buses that connect with railway lines and useful towns. Details are given at relevant points in the route description.

- **Three days** from Passo Gardena in Stage 4 (bus from Bolzano) to Passo San Pellegrino in Stage 6 (bus to Trento).
- **Four days** from Bressanone in Stage 1 (train) to Passo Gardena in Stage 4 (bus to Bolzano).
- **Four days** from Passo San Pellegrino in Stage 6 (bus from Trento or Belluno) to Passo Cereda in Stage 10 (bus to Feltre).
- **Six days** from Passo Gardena in Stage 4 (bus from Bolzano) to Rifugio Pradidali in Stage 9 (exit to Fiera di Primiero for bus to Feltre).

- **Ten days** from Bressanone in Stage 1 (train) to Passo Cereda in Stage 10 (bus to Feltre).

ACCOMMODATION

Walkers can look forward to a marvellous range of memorable places to stay and eat on the Alte Vie. All are listed with contact details in the route descriptions. Appendix A includes contact details for tourist offices, should you need more information.

Rifugi

An overnight stay in a Dolomites *rifugio* (*Hütte* in German, *Ücia* or *Ütia* in Ladin) is as essential as the walking experience. Cramped, rambling, cosy, modern, spartan… these hostel-like structures occupy amazing high-altitude spots. The majority belong to the Club Alpino Italiano (CAI) along with the Trento branch SAT and Südtirol AVS, but lots are run by local families and alpine guides. The first huts were the work of far-seeing pioneers back in the late 1800s when Dolomites mountaineering was in its heyday. Thankfully since modernised, throughout the summer months they provide accommodation for walkers and climbers as well as excellent home-cooked meals and drinks all day, often served in a timber-lined *stube* – a room warmed by a traditional tiled stove. A *custode* or guardian is in residence during the opening period (generally June to September) and a staff member is always on duty

Rifugio Pisciadù and its lovely lake (AV2, Stage 4)

to greet guests, deal with emergencies and satisfy needs – within reason. These jacks-of-all-trades also need to be good at chopping wood, baking cakes, speaking different languages and even transporting supplies by rucksack if there's no cableway.

After checking in, guests need to leave their boots on the racks near the front door and change into sandals or hut slippers. Sleeping quarters range from 2–4 bed or bunk rooms to a cavernous *dormitorio* (*Lager* in German). Duvets or blankets and a pillow are always provided, but guests must have their own sleeping sheet or bag liner – on sale in many huts. Smaller rooms with bed linen are sometimes available if you desire privacy – request a *camera*, but be aware that rooms *con bagno* (with en suite) are as rare as hen's teeth. Bathrooms are normally shared. Sparkling clean, they have hand basins, mirrors and toilet cubicles (loo paper is always provided). You will need your own towel. Don't always expect a hot shower – especially in late summer when water shortages lead to restrictions. When on offer, it will come at a price and is usually timed so be quick if you don't want to end up in a lather you can't rinse off! It is safe to assume a hot shower is available unless specified otherwise in the accommodation listings.

You may consider rinsing out your day's gear: hang items outside on

27

WATER

Water is relatively scarce throughout the Dolomites due to the porous dolomite and limestone rock – which implies that most surface water disappears underground – as well as the dearth of glaciers and permanent snowfields. The bottom line is: use it sparingly and don't take it for granted. Tap water is *acqua da rubinetto*. A general rule is to top up your bottle whenever possible. It may occasionally not be drinkable – *acqua non potabile* (*Kein Trinkwasser* in German); this is the case in all the Pale di San Martino huts. By all means, carry a sterilising filter – all shapes and sizes are available on the market. Mineral water is always on sale, although this inevitably involves polluting transport and plastic bottles.

the clothes line unless there happens to be a drying room. Hint: don't leave your washing outside overnight as it will be soaked by dew.

'Lights out' and silence are the rule between 10pm and 6am. The *rifugio* generator may be switched off, so keep your torch handy in case you need it during the night.

Meals are served at set times in a communal dining room that buzzes with mountain talk in different languages. Dinner is usually 7 or 7.30pm, so don't arrive late at a hut as you'll risk missing it! If you have special dietary requirements, give the staff advance notice so they can cater for you. Gluten-free is *senza glutine*, I'm vegetarian/vegan is *sono vegetariana/vegana* (or *vegetariano/vegano* for men). See the following section for food info.

No matter who a *rifugio* belongs to, anybody is welcome to stay – club membership is not compulsory. Rates vary according to the facilities offered.

An average of €55 will cover *mezza pensione*/half board (three-course dinner, overnight stay, breakfast) not counting drinks. It tends to be a good deal, although some saving can be made if you order individual meals. *Pernottamento* means an overnight stay with no food. In the club-run huts, members (*soci*) of CAI and affiliated UIAA associations can count on saving at least €10.

Carry a good supply of euros in cash; there is but a single ATM on AV2 (at Passo San Pellegrino, Stage 6) and detouring to a town takes up precious holiday time. Where possible, settle your bill in the evening to save wasting time in the morning. Some huts accept credit card payments, but check individual entries and never take it for granted.

Reservation is possible online as most huts have websites – a confirmation email is essential, and a deposit may be requested. Phone if in doubt. Full contact details can be found in

ALPINE CLUBS

Membership of the CAI (Club Alpino Italiano) is open to all nationalities. Intending members need to apply to individual branches; the complete list can be found at www.cai.it. The annual fee is around €50, with half-price rates for family members and 18–25 year olds, and less for children. As well as reductions in huts across the Alps, this covers alpine rescue insurance. Otherwise, Brits can join the UK branch of the Austrian club https://aacuk. org.uk, and for North Americans there's the Canadian club www.alpine clubofcanada.ca and the US organisation https://americanalpineclub.org.

the accommodation entries within the route description. Advance booking is strongly recommended for midsummer weekends. That said, some people only plan ahead two or three days at a time, phoning as they go. This is viable if you're versatile and prepared to use the mid-stage accommodation alternatives listed.

To phone from abroad, use the Italian country code +39 and include the initial '0' when dialling a landline. All of the refuges and hotels have a phone, occasionally only a mobile – recognisable by a number starting with '3'. An increasing number of places now offer Wi-Fi.

Rifugio Pradidali occupies an impressive position opposite Cima Canali (AV2, Stage 9)

Hotels

AV2 touches on several villages and road passes with reasonably priced hotels (listed in the walk description) for walkers who feel the need to treat themselves. These are handy for rest days and provide a nice break from dormitory life. *Gasthof* is German for guesthouse, and Italian variants include *albergo*, *locanda* and *pensione*.

Bivouac huts

In Italy a *bivacco* – also known as *casera* (hut) or *ricovero* (shelter) – is an unmanned structure, usually a basic metal cabin or a converted shepherds' or woodcutters' hut fitted out by a local CAI group. Unless otherwise specified, they are always open and can be used by anyone. Facilities range wildly; all have bunk beds but not necessarily mattresses. Blankets, stove and utensils are variables so intending users should carry a sleeping bag, food and some sort of cooker. If no water is on hand, there will usually be a sign for *acqua* (water) or *sorgente* (spring) pointing to the nearest source. Bivouac huts can be lifesavers in bad weather or emergencies, so users should always make sure the place is left in good condition with doors and windows closed, and any supplies replenished. Two of these come in handy as alternatives on AV2 (Stages 9 and 11); however, for AV3–6 they are essential due to the dearth of manned huts. Note: be aware that they cannot be booked and

can fill up, especially on midsummer weekends. Carrying a lightweight tent is probably not a bad idea.

Note: during the pandemic, CAI bivouac huts were officially closed for sanitary reasons; if you plan on staying in a bivouac, it's a good idea to check on its condition with the closest refuge.

Camping

The only campground on AV2 is at Malga Ciapela in Stage 6, and wild camping is not permitted in the parks traversed (Stages 2–4, 7–13) with offenders risking hefty fines. It's marginally more feasible on AV3–6. Generally speaking, if you're prepared to carry the extra weight of tent, sleeping bag and cooking gear along with supplementary water and food, a pitch under the stars can be magical. However, don't forget that level terrain is at a premium in the Dolomites and these are not strolls; you need to be fit and experienced for long ascents and testing descents in alpine environments shouldering a cumbersome rucksack. To camp in the vicinity of a *rifugio*, check with the staff first; if allowed, they'll usually suggest a good spot. Wherever you camp be discreet, follow the 'dusk to dawn' rule and leave no trace.

With the exception of Malga Ciapela, there are no grocery shops along AV2 and unless you use the huts for meals and snacks, replenishing food supplies is not an easy task, requiring time-consuming detours using the exit routes given.

FOOD AND DRINK

Meals are important in the day of a walker. All the *rifugi* along the way provide meals, snacks and refreshments, so you don't need to weigh yourself down with huge amounts of food.

Colazione or breakfast is generally continental style, with *caffè latte* (milk coffee) or *tè* (tea) to accompany bread, butter and jam, although cereals and yogurt, ham (*prosciutto*), cheese (*formaggio*) and eggs (*uova*) are increasingly on offer.

If you need a picnic lunch, staff are always happy to prepare rolls (*panini*) – but get your order in the evening before. Otherwise, factor in lunch at an establishment en route. The menu will be similar to the evening meal, as follows.

Dinner (*cena*) usually means a choice of a first course (*primo piatto*), such as soup with vegetables (*minestrone*) or barley (*zuppa d'orzo*). There's always pasta with a meat (*ragù*) or tomato (*al pomodoro*) sauce. Specialities include *gnocchi di patate con ricotta affumicata*, tiny delicate potato dumplings with smoked cheese; and *casunziei*, soft ravioli with a beetroot filling and poppy seeds. *Canederli* are savoury bread dumplings flavoured with speck (smoked ham) and chives and

The cosy dining room at Rifugio Castiglioni (AV2, Stage 5)

served in consommé or with melted butter.

Second course tends to be meat: *manzo* is beef, *maiale* pork, and *vitello* veal; *tagliata* is a type of steak. The flavoursome peppery sausage *pastin* hails from the southern Dolomites, as does *schiz* aka *tosèla*, a fresh local cheese like mozzarella that is grilled or pan-fried in butter and cream.

Polenta is common: thick, steaming-hot cornmeal served with spicy meat stew goulash, *funghi* (wild mushrooms) or *formaggio fuso* (melted cheese). Unbeatable. A *frittata* (omelette) is an alternative, as are *uova con speck e patate* (fried eggs with speck and potatoes). Vegetables generally come as side dishes; fresh salad if you're lucky.

Dessert may be *frutti di bosco* (wild berries), served with cake or ice cream. Other guaranteed standards are homemade *crostata* fruit tart or *Apfelstrudel*, a luscious thin pastry case filled with sliced apple and spices. *Kaiserschmarrn* is a scrumptious Südtirol concoction of sliced pancake with sultanas and spread with jam – a meal in itself. Look out for *Zelten*, a rich biscuit crammed with dried fruit; it travels well in rucksacks.

Soft drinks and beer are widely available as are some memorable local wines. The reds include full-bodied Teroldego and lighter Schiava from the Trentino, then excellent Lagrein and Blauburgunder (Pinot Nero) from the slopes around Bolzano. The list of whites is headed by aromatic Gewürztraminer, while very drinkable Rieslings are grown on the slopes above the Isarco valley.

Lastly come fiery home-brewed *grappas* served after dinner and flavoured with bilberries, sultanas, pine resin and unbelievably bitter gentian root. Don't forget you have to get up and go walking tomorrow!

WHAT TO TAKE

You will need far less than you think. Basic items for personal comfort and gear to cover all weather extremes are essential, but be strict with yourself and remember you'll have to lug your stuff over the mountains for days on end. Safety is paramount: a heavy rucksack can become a hazard, putting tired walkers off-balance and leading to unpleasant falls and serious accidents. Do you really need that paperback or weighty tablet? The 10pm 'lights out' rule in huts precludes bedtime reading, and meal times can be profitable for trying out your language skills with other walkers and swapping track experiences.

The following checklist should help:

- comfortable boots with ankle support and non-slip Vibram-type sole
- rucksack – 35-litre capacity should do; plastic or stuff bags for separating contents
- light footwear such as sandals for evenings

- layers of clothing for dealing with conditions from scorching sun to a snow storm: t-shirts and shorts, comfortable long trousers (not jeans), warm fleece, a woolly hat and gloves (handy on cabled stretches)
- waterproofs – jacket, over-trousers and rucksack cover, or a poncho
- whistle, small headlamp or torch for calling for help
- lightweight sleeping sheet – silk is perfect
- small towel + personal toiletries
- mini first-aid kit and essential medicines
- high-energy snack food such as muesli bars
- maps and guidebook
- supply of euros in cash and credit/debit card
- telescopic trekking poles to help wonky knees on steep descents
- sunglasses, hat, chapstick and high-factor cream. For every 1000m you climb, the intensity of the sun's UV rays increases by 10%, augmented by reflection on snow. This, combined with lower levels of humidity and pollution which act as filters in other places, means you need a much higher protection factor cream than at sea level.
- water bottle or similar
- mobile phone, charger with adaptor
- camera, charger with adaptor

- foam ear plugs – they occupy next to no space and ensure a good night's sleep in a dormitory with snorers.
- ice axe and crampons – very occasionally needed in early summer if there is icy hard snow on the Sella and San Martino plateaus (contact the relevant refuges to check before packing your rucksack).

AV2 has aided stretches of varying lengths and difficulty – see stages 3, 4, 5, 7, 8, 9, 11 and 12. Less confident walkers may consider carrying a sling for the waist and karabiners for reassurance without the bulk of the full via ferrata set, although be aware that these do not spell total protection and safety.

Long chunks of AV4, AV5 and AV6 are full-blooded via ferrata routes and require the appropriate experience and/or a qualified guide, as well as the following gear that must conform to UIAA (Union Internationale des Associations d'Alpinisme) standards:

- helmet for protection against falling stones. Remember: it's only effective if it's strapped to your head and not your rucksack.
- full body harness and Y-model ferrata kit comprising belay ropes, karabiners and a shock absorber.

MAPS AND WAYMARKING

The maps in this book, at a scale of 1:75,000, show the route location

and give information about important landmarks and geographical features. The map booklet (1:25,000) that accompanies this guide gives more detail.

As an alternative to the Kompass maps in the included map booklet, the Tabacco 1:25,000 *carta topografica per escursionisti* are also excellent. They can be consulted and ordered at www.tabaccoeditrice.it as well as bookshops in Italy and overseas. Tabacco's app for digital maps is downloadable at https://tabacco mapp.it.

With slight overlaps, the following sheets are needed for AV2:

• 030 *Bressanone/Brixen Val di Funes/Villnöss* for Stages 1–3
• 07 *Alta Badia-Arabba-Marmolada* for Stages 3–5

• 015 *Marmolada-Pelmo-Civetta-Moiazza* for Stages 6–7
• 022 *Pale di San Martino* for Stages 8–12
• 023 *Alpi Feltrine-Le Vette-Cimònega* for Stages 12–13.

For Alte Vie 3–6, the relevant Kompass 1:35,000 and Tabacco 1:25,000 sheet maps are listed in the individual information boxes at the beginning of each trek.

The glossary in Appendix B includes terminology found on maps.

Waymarking for the AV2 is '2' in a red triangle, but where this is faded or missing, you need to follow the local path numbers given in the route description and on maps. All paths have an identifying number and the official CAI waymarking – red/white bars painted on prominent landmarks

Waymarking for Alta Via 2

such as outcrops or trees, as well as signposts.

DOS AND DON'TS

It's better to arrive early and dry, than late and wet.
Maxim for long-distance walkers

- Find time to get into good shape before setting out on your holiday, as it will maximise enjoyment. Remember that you'll be walking on alpine terrain which is never level, often steep and rocky, and exposed in places. You'll appreciate the scenery more if you're fit and healthy, and you'll react better in an emergency.
- Choose your footwear carefully. Avoid brand-new footwear (blisters!), but leave worn-out boots at home (slippery!).
- Apply the golden rule for rucksack preparation: 10% of your body weight + 2kg. Weigh in on the bathroom scales. Do make allowances for drinking-water and food, and keep in mind that as the afternoon wears on and

that hut seems ever further away, your pack will inexplicably get heavier.
- Carry extra protective clothing as well as energy foods for emergency situations. Remember that in normal circumstances the temperature drops an average of 6°C for every 1000m you climb.
- Don't be overambitious. Read the walk description before setting out and factor in a rest day if necessary.
- Don't set out late and always have extra time up your sleeve to allow for detours due to collapsed bridges, wrong turns and missing signposts. Plan on getting to your destination at an early hour in hot weather, as afternoon storms are not uncommon.
- Stick with your companions and don't lose sight of them. Remember that the progress of the group matches that of the slowest member.
- Preferably, don't walk solo. While it can be a very special experience, remember it exposes you to more risk in case of a mishap.
- Learn the international call for help (see below).
- Check the weather forecast when possible – hut guardians are in the know. For the Südtirol see https://weather.provinz.bz.it, for Trentino see www.meteotrentino.it, and for the Veneto consult www.arpa.veneto.it. Never set out if conditions are bad. Even a

The final aided sections before Pian dei Cantoni on Alta Via 2 (Stage 8)

broad track can become treacherous in adverse weather, and high-altitude terrain enveloped in thick mist makes orientation difficult. In electrical storms, don't shelter under trees or rock overhangs and keep away from metallic fixtures.

- Check out the advice from the CAI experts at www.montagna micaesicura.it.

- Carry rubbish to a bin where it can be disposed of correctly; please don't push it under a rock. Organic waste such as apple cores and orange peel should not be left lying around as it upsets the diet of animals and birds.

- Be considerate when making a toilet stop. Abandoned huts and rock overhangs could serve as life-saving shelter for someone. If you must use paper or tissues, carry it away; the small lightweight bags used by dog owners

are perfect. There is no excuse for leaving unsightly toilet paper anywhere.

- Collecting flowers, insects or minerals is strictly forbidden everywhere, as is lighting fires.

- The Dolomites are in Italy – so make an effort to learn some Italian. All efforts will be hugely appreciated.

- Remember to collect the inked stamps from the *rifugi* you visit and present them to the Feltre tourist office at the end of AV2 for a badge and congratulations!

EMERGENCIES

For medical matters, walkers who live in the EU need a European Health Insurance Card (EHIC) while UK residents require a UK Global Health Insurance Card (GHIC). Holders of each are entitled to free or subsidised emergency treatment in Italy, which has an excellent public health system. Australia has a reciprocal agreement – see www.medicareaustralia.gov.au. Those from other countries should make sure they have appropriate coverage.

Travel insurance to cover an alpine walking holiday is also strongly recommended, as costs in the case of rescue and repatriation can be hefty. Most alpine clubs cover their members for rescue operations – see box in 'Accommodation'.

Aiuto! (pronounced 'eye-yoo-toh') in Italian, and *Zu Hilfe!* (pronounced 'tsoo hilfer') in German, mean Help!

The international rescue signals can come in handy: the call for help is **six** signals per minute. These can be visual (such as waving a handkerchief or flashing a torch) or audible (whistling or shouting). Repeat after a one-minute pause. The answer is **three** visual or audible signals per minute, to be repeated after a one-minute pause. Anyone who sees or hears a call for help must contact the nearest *rifugio* or police station as quickly as possible.

In Italy, the general emergency telephone number is 112, while calls for *soccorso alpino* (mountain rescue) need to be made to 118.

A final note, on mobile phones: it is tempting to be lulled into a false sense of security when carrying a mobile phone in the mountains. Be aware that relatively few high-alpine places have a signal. In contrast, all *rifugi* have a landline, mobile or satellite phone, and experienced staff can always be relied on in emergencies.

USING THIS GUIDE

This guide divides AV2 into 13 handy stages that correspond to a reasonable day's walking, concluding at a *rifugio* with meals and accommodation. However, these are only suggestions, and the abundance of huts along the trek means you can often vary stages and overnight stops.

Throughout the route description, useful landmarks that feature on the accompanying stage map are given in **bold** with intermediary timing and altitude.

The info box at the beginning of each stage contains the following essential information:

Distance in kilometres. (This is nowhere near as important as height gain or loss.)

Total ascent in metres (NB 100m=328ft)

Total descent in metres

Grade gives an idea of the difficulty of the stage. Remember that adverse weather conditions or snow cover will increase this. The grades used in this guide are as follows:

- **1:** a straightforward path with moderate gradient, suitable for all walkers (this corresponds to the Italian 'T', *Turistico*)
- **2:** a fairly strenuous alpine walk, but not especially difficult ('E', *Escursionistico* in Italian)

Evening light from Rifugio Mulaz (AV2, Stage 7)

- **3:** experience on mountainous terrain is a prerequisite as there may be particularly steep and exposed sections; a head for heights and orientation skills will come in useful ('EE', *Escursionistico esperto* in Italian).

In terms of average overall difficulty, the AV2 and AV3 rate Grade 2–3, while AV4–6 are Grade 3.

Time is approximate and does not include pauses for picnics, admiring views, photos and toilet stops. These are skeleton times, so always add on a couple of hours to be realistic. Everyone walks at a different pace.

GPX tracks

GPX tracks for the AV2 route in this guidebook are available to download free at www.cicerone.co.uk/1097/GPX. If you have not bought the book through the Cicerone website, or have bought the book without opening an account, please register your purchase in your Cicerone library to access GPX and update information.

A GPS device is an excellent aid to navigation, but you should also carry a map and compass and know how to use them. GPX files are provided in good faith, but in view of the profusion of formats and devices, neither the author nor the publisher accepts responsibility for their use. We provide files in a single standard GPX format that works on most devices and systems, but you may need to convert files to your preferred format using a GPX converter such as GPS Visualizer or one of the many other apps and online converters available.

ALTA VIA 2

Vast views over Val Badia from the path to Passo Poma (Stage 2)

The porticoed streets of Bressanone

The elegant Tyrolean town of Bressanone/Brixen is a marvellous starting point for the superb Alta Via 2 (AV2) long-distance traverse of the Dolomites. Standing at the confluence of the Rienza and Isarco rivers, whose waters blend with the mighty Adige further south, it is easily reached from either Austria or northern Italy by rail or road. The charming traffic-free centre is worth a wandering visit for its porticoed streets and Gothic and baroque architecture – including the 18th-century cathedral with its soaring spire. Bressanone's Palazzo Vescovile (bishops' residence) boasts a delightful collection of traditional Christmas cribs and nativity scenes, with ornate figures hundreds of years old.

The town is also an excellent place to stock up on food at the open-air markets, inviting bakeries, delis and supermarkets. Apart from the first village on the way up, San Andrea, this is your only chance to shop until Malga Ciapela in Stage 6.

In addition to a helpful tourist office (tel 0472 275252, www.brixen. org), it has a great range of hotel accommodation as well as a centrally located youth hostel (tel 0472 279999, www.jugendherberge.bz).

STAGE 1
Bressanone to Rifugio Plose

Start	Bressanone
Distance	12km
Total ascent	1910m
Total descent	20m
Grade	2
Time	5hr 45min (can be shortened to 1hr 15min + bus/lifts)

Starting out from valley level, AV2 makes its way through farming villages to higher spectacular reaches well away from the hustle and bustle. The destination is the Plose, a nondescript mountain well known to winter skiers and mountain bikers, and (of greater interest to AV2 walkers) home to a superbly appointed *rifugio*. It's a perfect first night out on the trek, offering unrivalled views onto the northernmost Dolomites.

A short stretch along tarmac gives way to lovely paths and meadows, then forest for a long, long climb – which can, however, be shortened. In fact, non-purists will appreciate the bus as well as the gondola car to ease the 1900+m height gain demanded by this opening stage: SAD buses from the railway station run via St Andrea to the departure station of the Plose Seilbahn lift (June to early October) that whisks you up to Valcroce for a link with the main route. The final section traverses open heathland, where panoramas are non-stop through 360 degrees.

No particular difficulty is encountered, although the massive height gain should not be underrated.

From the railway station at **Bressanone** (561m), the street Mozartallee leads due E across the grey-green Isarco river to a T-intersection where you fork R, as per signs for Plose. (If you detour by way of the town centre, from the main square head E for the river and a minor bridge, then turn R to reach this spot – allow an extra 30min).

After 1.3km walking S along the road, branch L on n.4A at a fountain and onto Kirchsteig. Red/white stripes guide you past apple orchards to an old church (**Maria am Sand**, 620m) where you go L across a stream. A little

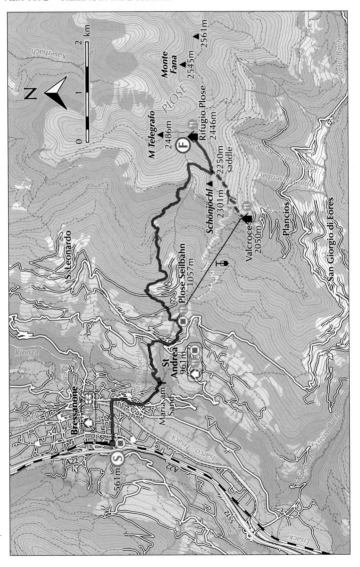

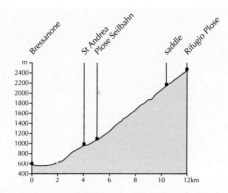

further uphill, the path (n.4A) veers sharp L, climbing through chestnut and pine wood, then fields and farms. It joins the road briefly as you approach **St Andrea** (961m, **1hr 15min**). ▸

In the village centre, on the corner of Hotel Gasserhof and its inviting beer garden, turn uphill on n.4, which threads its way past houses old and new, their window boxes spilling geraniums. A final wander through woodland brings you to the bus stop at the **Plose Seilbahn** lift departure station (1057m, **15min**) and a difficult decision – to walk, or to ride the gondola car...

SAD buses, hotels, groceries, tourist info (tel 0472 850008).

Gondola car variant
You alight from the lift at **Valcroce**/Kreuztal (2050m). Only metres away from the arrival station is beautifully placed café-restaurant-guesthouse Pension Geisler (tel 0472 521319, www.pension-geisler.it).

Turn L for the straightforward climb NE past ski lifts and pistes through shrubby vegetation of heather and cowberries, with cows and sheep at pasture. Keep R below **Schönjöchl** to reach a **saddle** (2250m) and the main route.

On foot, take the clearly signed n.4 path through the gondola car buildings then steadily uphill through woods and the occasional field, heading mostly NE at first.

Along with carpets of bilberries, a couple of farm roads and lanes are crossed as the way bears ESE. After intersecting n.30, you find yourself above the tree line and soon veer R, climbing to a high ridge where the brilliant line-up of the Odle di Eores is revealed along with bird's-eye views over Bressanone. At a **saddle** (2250m) close to Schönjöchl, keep L (NE) on n.7 – joined by the route from Valcroce and the gondola lift.

The final puff-inducing 200 metres uphill follow a narrowing path that concludes almost vertically at the white refuge building (2446m, **4hr 15min**).

> **Rifugio Plose** aka Plosehütte (tel 0472 521333, **www.plosehuette.com**, CAI, sleeps 60, open early June to late Oct, accepts credit cards). Modern bar/restaurant designed for winter skiers, but summer guests are fed well and get to stay in cosy timber-lined sleeping quarters.

There is a magnificent outlook here to the jagged barrier of the Odle di Eores, aptly named in Ladin for 'needles'. Southeast is twin-peaked Sass de Putia while southwest rises Sassolungo flanked by the Sciliar massif. Quite amazing! Find time for the short stroll to nearby 2486m Monte Telegrafo, sprouting a clutter of aerials and a helpful *Rundpanoramatisch* (orientation table) that identifies all those rocky points.

The magnificent outlook to the Odle di Eores at stage end

STAGE 2
Rifugio Plose to Rifugio Genova

Start	Rifugio Plose
Distance	13.5km
Total ascent	680m
Total descent	530m
Grade	2
Time	4hr

A magnificent stage with straightforward walking and breathtaking views. Once the ski zone of Plose is left behind, woodland with a wealth of elegant arolla pine is traversed. Then AV2 enters the Parco Naturale Puez-Odle for a stiff climb. This concludes at a pass opening onto pasture upland where the destination hut stands, a comfortable place serving traditional Südtirol fare. Today a couple of café-restaurants are touched on – lovely spots for a drink, meal or alternative overnight stay.

The relative brevity of this stage means you can take it easy. On the other hand, if you have time, allow for the highly recommended optional 2hr return ascent of 2875m Sass de Putia. The northernmost of the Dolomite peaks, it boasts record-making views to 449 church spires across the region – binoculars are a help.

Leave **Rifugio Plose** (2446m) on n.4, following a fence with a stunning outlook to the snowbound Italo-Austrian border. In gentle descent the path passes ski lifts and then changes direction abruptly a couple of times, heading essentially S over grassy slopes. It cuts across a dirt road and heads into woodland thick with alpenrose and bilberry shrubs watered by trickling streams.

Several lengths of guiding cable accompany stretches (no exposure) cut into the mountainside and over a footbridge. You emerge on meadows dotted with photogenic timber chalets and quickly join a dirt road (turn L) close to **Kerer Kreuzl** (2000m) with an artistic wooden crucifix.

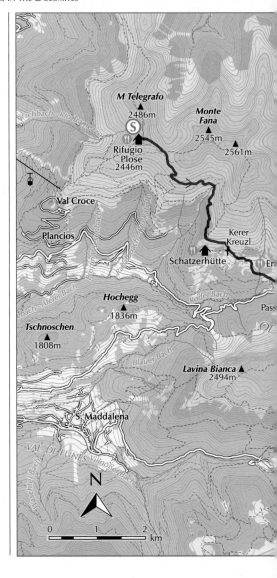

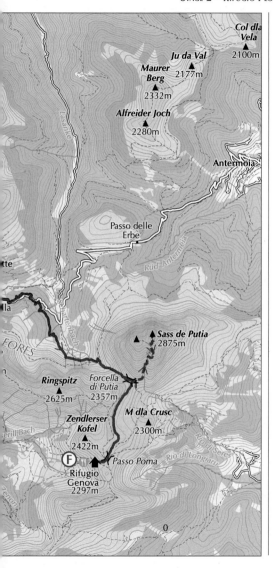

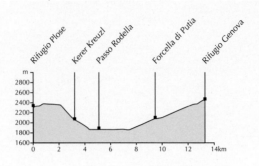

Passo Rodella is the divider between the Plose and the Putia mountain groups.

Above loom the impressive Odle di Eores.

Close by is charming **Schatzerhütte** (meals and accommodation, tel 0472 521343, www. schatzerhuette.com, open May to Nov).

Not far along, n.4 branches R (SE) through woodland, bypassing eatery **Enzianhütte**. In sight of the road, keep L for boardwalks across marshy terrain thick with cottongrass to the road at **Passo Rodella** aka Halsl (1886m, **1hr 30min**) and the Rodelalm farm-cum-café. ◀

Keep L to where n.4 drops L to avoid the traffic, staying parallel to the road for a short spell and rejoining it close to a key fork R off the tarmac. Here, AV2 enters the Puez-Odle park. Heading constantly SSE, a good path coasts through woodland and over a stream for a narrow passage below a waterfall – watch your step. ◀

The path enters the gully leading to Forcella di Putia for a relentless climb SE over broken rock and cascading watercourses. Walkers are dwarfed by the awesome west face of Sass de Putia, its lower layers a fascinating lesson in geology. Several paths join up and you move to the L side of the gully at a giant boulder. Zigzags with timber reinforcements help the ascent, although these may be buried as snow lies late here.

You finally emerge at **Forcella di Putia** (2357m, **2hr**) with a crucifix and welcoming benches. After all the scree, the vast pastureland here offers a dramatic

Walkers take a rest at Forcella di Putia

contrast, complete with a gorgeous outlook east to Sasso della Croce and Cunturines over Val Badia. ▶

Ascent of Sass de Putia (2hr return)

Sharp L from Forcella di Putia is the path leading into the central fold of Sass de Putia, where a shallow gully-valley often harbours late-lying snow. Wide curves climb steadily – keep R at a fork for a brief crest passage to a broad saddle at 2760m. Here, tackle the final cable-aided stretch via an exposed shoulder and hands-on climb to the 2875m summit of **Sass de Putia**. Should that not appeal, turn L (W) at the saddle for the easy route to the twin peak, Piccolo Sass de Putia, only metres lower. The views are quite amazing and range 360 degress, taking in a vast selection of Dolomites along with the northern snow-capped Austrian Alps. ▶ Return the same way to Forcella di Putia.

Now, a mostly level path heads off S over grassy flowered panoramic slopes, to **Passo Poma** (2340m). Only a short flight of steps R is **Rifugio Genova** (2297m, **30min**).

Rifugio Genova aka Schlüterhütte (tel 0472 670072 or 347 2667694, www.schlueterhuette.com,

Ahead to the south is the many-turreted Puez-Odle massif – tomorrow's destination.

Tame alpine choughs keep you company.

The stage concludes at Rifugio Genova

sleeps 90, open mid June to mid Oct). A lovely, rambling timber building inaugurated in 1898, it was constructed by a councillor from Dresden and donated to the DÖAV, the Austro-German Alpine Club. Once run by the Genoese branch of CAI, it is now the property of the Bolzano province. It's a lively, popular place run by an extended local family who excel in fragrant homemade cakes among other tasty dishes.

STAGE 3
Rifugio Genova to Rifugio Puez

Start	Rifugio Genova
Distance	12km
Total ascent	840m
Total descent	660m
Grade	2–3
Time	5hr

A spectacular long traverse with brilliant views all day. After contouring flowered pasture slopes you embark on a fatiguing climb, followed by a drawn-out series of ups and downs – and an aided stretch, tricky but short. As a fitting reward you venture onto the unworldly Puez plateau, a vast undulating *altopiano* scarce in terms of plant life but rich in fossils. The upper rock layer has eroded into bizarre monumental 'sculptures'. The last leg today crosses the head of the awesome Vallunga, a glacially sculpted U-shaped trough. This brilliant stage is brought to its close at a friendly family-run hut. If you're hankering after a hotel room, continue on to Passo Gardena – a further 2hr 45min – see Stage 4.

En route is an optional short via ferrata (only for experts with gear and no vertigo problems) that cuts 1hr off the stage.

From **Rifugio Genova** (2297m) path n.3 strikes out uphill, SE at first, to cut around the **Bronsoi** knoll over flowered slopes. A stretch due S leads to an amazingly panoramic col at 2421m where the Puez group rears ahead, not to mention the Seceda giant and the Odle. Veering SW, you amble past marmot colonies and detour briefly via Medalares Alm (2293m, refreshments), to reach the minor pass of **Kreuzjoch** (2293m).

Approaching the Odle and Piz Duleda, the path proceeds due S over a vast wooded valley head dominated by scree flows. Dodging a couple of outcrops, it moves onto a scree base for interminable zigzags and late-lying

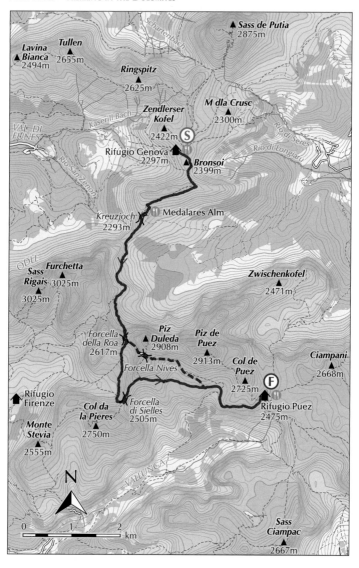

It's a steep scree ascent to Forcella della Roa

snow to gain **Forcella della Roa** (2617m, **2hr 30min**) – a broad saddle and hangout of hungry choughs. ▶

Forcella Nives via ferrata variant
From Forcella della Roa go L to take the narrow path 2c which hugs the cliffs to reach a gully for the partially

The brilliant outlook includes tempting glimpses of the Sella ahead.

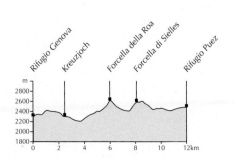

53

aided clamber up a rock face. It emerges at **Forcella Nives** (2740m) then you head ESE over gentle slopes to rejoin the main route before Rifugio Puez.

From Forcella della Roa it's an easy descent straight into a chaotic amphitheatre. Not far down, take care not to miss the fork L where AV2 parts ways from n.3 (which continues down to Rifugio Firenze). The clear path picks its way across shattered rock and yellow poppies to where it links with n.2 (from Rifugio Firenze). It's a puff-inducing climb E to **Forcella di Sielles** (2505m, **1hr**) set dizzily above steep-sided Vallunga.

Now cable-aided stretches with a little exposure lead L up the adjoining crest, reaching 2590m, before a narrow scree path proceeds to ample grassy slopes. Veering E, the route meanders over pasture appreciated by chomping sheep, and basins bright with a riot of rock campion and forget-me-not. After the variant joins up you pass a path fork (for Santa Cristina) at the head of the mighty Vallunga. Then a gentle uphill stretch continues to the hut, visible at the very last moment (2475m, **1hr 30min**).

> **Rifugio Puez** (tel 0474 646427, **www.rifugiopuez. it**, CAI, sleeps 85, open mid June to end Sept). The refuge's isolated situation, far from jeep tracks and lacking a mechanised cableway, means supplies have to be brought in by helicopter. A clean and efficient establishment dating from 1982, it swarms with day walkers who appreciate the delicious strudel and luscious hot chocolate. The original 1889 hut stands nearby.

STAGE 4
Rifugio Puez to Rifugio Pisciadù

Start	Rifugio Puez
Distance	10km
Total ascent	900m
Total descent	800m
Grade	3
Time	5hr

Today's opener is a delightful meander continuing across the Puez plateau, which is embedded with fossilised ammonites and megalodon shells similar to deer hoofprints. The pretty lakes dotting the surface were a source of fear in olden times as dragons reportedly slumbered in their depths! A descent concludes at one of the most beautiful Dolomite road passes – Passo Gardena, a lovely spot to stay if desired. Connecting Ladin-speaking Val Gardena and Val Badia, it has the bonus of accommodation and buses; however, for walkers on the AV2 it represents the gateway to the Sella group – a unique, awe-inspiring massif akin to a fortress that stands isolated. Originally a coral atoll, its sheer forbidding flanks and terraces are recognisable from afar.

A dramatic gully slices deep into the Sella, entailing hands-on clambering and cable-aided passages, earning the stage its Grade 3 difficulty. It all concludes at a top-class *rifugio* on a superb high-altitude platform.

It's inadvisable to embark on the ascent to Rifugio Pisciadù late in the day or in unsettled weather; even in good conditions you can expect to encounter huge numbers of climbers descending Val Setus on their return from vie ferrate. If in doubt, stay over at Passo Gardena and start out early next morning.

From **Rifugio Puez** (2475m), the well-trodden n.2 passes the hut's flagpole and skirts the head of Vallunga where

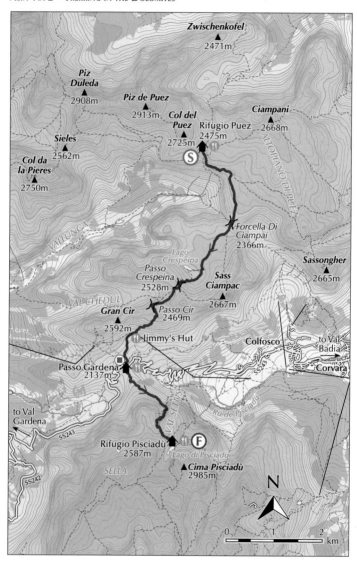

views extend southwest to the Sciliar. It continues across the fascinating *altopiano* punctuated with curious volcano-like mounds. Needless to say, the outlook is vast – but remember to keep a lookout downward for fossils.

After a stretch S towards the Sassongher, the path passes through a short gully with timber reinforcements, veering sharp R past **Forcella di Ciampai** (2366m). Keep straight on (SW), dipping through grassy basins and across streams not far from the green water of

On the way to Passo Crespeina

The dramatic flanks of the Sella on the way to Val Setus

Lago Crespeina, an inviting picnic spot. Beneath Sass Ciampac, zigzags lead up to **Passo Crespeina** (2528m, **1hr 30min**) and its artistic crucifix. Here you bid farewell to the *altopiano*.

With a decent view southwest to Sassolungo, the path descends steeply into the head of Val Chedul, passes a path for Selva and crawls L over broken rubble across to **Passo Cir** (2469m), where weird and wonderful eroded rock spires reminiscent of totem poles abound. You meander through a jungle of pinnacles, emerging to awesome views of the Sella, close at hand now.

SAD buses run down both sides of the pass – to Val Badia as well as Val Gardena.

The path continues down through dwarf mountain pines and past the chalet eatery **Jimmy's Hütte** in the shade of the Gran Cir, to a gravel track. This concludes at **Passo Gardena** (2137m, **1hr 15min**) and the welcoming Rifugio Berghaus Frara. ◄

Rifugio Berghaus Frara (tel 0471 795225, **www. rifugiofrara.it**, sleeps 40 in dorm and rooms, open late June to end Sept, credit cards accepted).

However, tarry not as a stiff climb still awaits walkers intent on finishing this stage today.

Alongside Berghaus Frara, take path n.666, which climbs straight up a grass-earth crest then bears L (SE) through shrubby vegetation at the foot of soaring cliffs. After half an hour the yawning mouth to wild Val Setus is reached. ▸ AV2 forks R (S) for the steep assault up this awesome ravine of mobile scree and stone rubble, often harbouring snow well into summer.

The name Val Setus derives from 'haymaker', for the lush meadows below.

With the sound of traffic on the snaking road dimming below, you ascend steadily on well-marked regular curves, keeping to the right-hand side – out of the way of the odd rockfall from higher chutes. A fair way up, the path veers L across a gully for an aided stretch fitted with iron rungs, spikes and a thick cable attached to the rock face. Take your time. Exposure is medium and there are plentiful footholds, but it will be around half an hour before you climb out onto the spectacular terrace beneath Sass da Lech. Phew!

Branch L for the short stroll to **Rifugio Pisciadù** (2587m, **2hr 15min**).

Rifugio Pisciadù aka Rifugio Franco Cavazza (tel 0471 836292, **www.rifugiopisciadu.it**, CAI, sleeps 104, open end June to end Sept, credit cards accepted). This very pleasant, modern, roomy hut is well run and occupies an incredible platform, looking down to the township of Colfosco far, far below.

The nearby tarn, Lago di Pisciadù, supplies both the refuge and a nearby waterfall, which gave its name to many landforms here. Bathing is forbidden.

STAGE 5
Rifugio Pisciadù to Rifugio Castiglioni

Start	Rifugio Pisciadù
Distance	16km
Total ascent	690m
Total descent	1230m
Grade	3
Time	6hr 30min

This is an awesome stage, covering an incredible variety of landscapes – ranging from the stark Sella to the lush flowered slopes of volcanic origin on the historic Viel del Pan, and to the immense glaciated Marmolada. It makes for a rather lengthy day, but if desired it can easily be split into less tiring chunks thanks to the string of refuges and hotels en route.

First off today, AV2 climbs further up the terraces of the majestic Sella to a vast lunar upland inhabited by ibex and choughs. Cairns, pole markers and red arrows painted on the ground show the way to a welcoming *rifugio*. Here, an optional ascent of popular walker's peak Piz Boè (3152m) is on the cards. Simply spectacular, it involves an extra 1hr 20min and approximately 250m height gain/loss. Then it's a plunge (or cable-car) to a road pass where hotels and buses can be found.

Thereafter is an easy path with brilliant views of the 3342m Marmolada, the loftiest mountain in the Dolomites. Geological interest is high as a vast volcanic intrusion is followed – perfect for prolific wildflowers. This so-called Viel del Pan ('the way of bread') was once used by grain smugglers to avoid hefty taxes imposed by the Venetian Republic. Restored in the late 1800s, it is also known as the Bindelweg after a former president of the DÖAV. After a short drop to a manmade lake, the day concludes at a historic refuge.

From **Rifugio Pisciadù** (2587m), signposts for n.666 point you S, skirting the lake. The path climbs slowly, cutting across scree falls from the yellowish west flank of Cima Pisciadù. You bear L to a short aided rock passage then

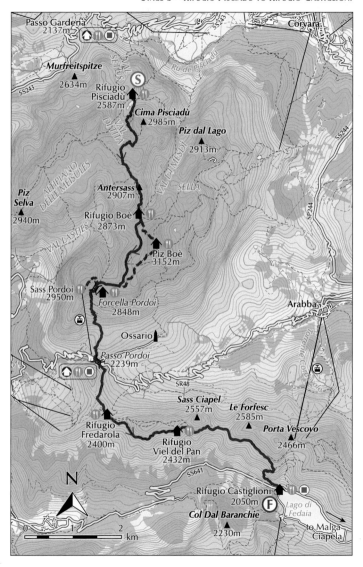

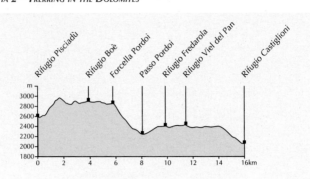

climb into debris-filled **Val di Tita**, where snow patches inevitably abound. In a squelchy hollow ignore the turn-off for Cima Pisciadù and keep R for more gentle climbing via a narrow gully.

Up at the 2900m mark is a rough platform with sweeping views over the vast Altipiano delle Meisules – a stone desert where ibex find enough summer sustenance to thrive. The elegant, rounded Sass Pordoi with its sheer sides is virtually straight ahead; the arrival station of the cable-car from Passo Pordoi perched on its peak. South is Piz Boè, its repeater mast and hut clinging on tight.

Next is an easy descent to a flat zone and path junction (which you ignore) for Val Lasties. ◀ Nearby L, in the proximity of towering Torre Berger, you get unnervingly dramatic glimpses down plunging Val di Mesdì. Now you need path n.647 for the climb S to 2907m on the **Antersass** – the highest point reached on AV2 – before a gentle slope drops to **Rifugio Boè** (2873m, 2hr 30min).

Val Lasties was long believed to be the dwelling place of witches.

Rifugio Boè (tel 0471 847303, **https:// en.rifugioboe.it**, CAI-SAT, sleeps 80, open late June to end Sept). A rambling establishment where a warm welcome is extended to walkers who venture onto this desolate landscape. The original building was erected in 1898 by the far-sighted

Bamberg branch of the DÖAV, but it was devastated during WW1. SAT, the Trento CAI branch, saw to its reconstruction and has recently undertaken superb modern extensions.

Weather and visibility permitting, a detour to neighbouring Piz Boè is thoroughly recommended. All effort is adequately repaid by the extraordinary views.

Variant via Piz Boè

Path n.638 heads uphill mostly SE, making its way across scree. It heads for a prominent bastion and an aided stretch traversing R which can prove difficult in icy conditions. The crest of awe-inspiring **Piz Boè** (3152m, **1hr**) hosts a radio mast and the cosy wooden hut Capanna Fassa (tel 0462 601723 or 336 452523, www.rifugiocapannapizfassa.com, sleeps 22, open mid June to late Sept, no shower). Use your map and compass (or app) to identify those mountains!

A little easier than the ascent, the descent route n.638 follows a ridge SW, scrambling down the outward corner. At its base a clear path continues in the same direction to join the main AV2 route from Rifugio Boè.

Heading S from Rifugio Boè across the undulating rock upland, path n.627 crosses well-trodden snow patches. It cuts across scree flows from Piz Boè, including curious red boulders. Cairns, poles and waymarks need to be followed carefully across the undulating terrain to a series of ledges studded with fossilised shells. The path from Piz Boè links in for the final leg coasting W to **Forcella Pordoi** (2848m, **40min**) and the dauntingly positioned Rifugio Forcella Pordoi.

Rifugio Forcella Pordoi (tel 366 7446715, www.rifugioforcellapordoi.com, sleeps 30 in dorm and rooms, open late June to Oct). It took 580 helicopter trips to transport the material needed for this chalet! A great place to stay.

AV2 traverses the stark Sella upland

Extension to Sass Pordoi

For more views (had enough yet?) or a restful cable-car trip down to Passo Pordoi, embark on the wide well-trodden path above the building for the final 100m uphill to the marvellous belvedere and restaurant on **Sass Pordoi** (2950m, **15min**) and then the mechanised descent.

From Forcella Pordoi, the 600m plunge to the road pass goes directly down that giddy gully L. There is nearly always snow at the top – or even ice – so take extra special care early in the season. Steps lead down the initial steep part to easy zigzags, where scree running is feasible. ◄

The dangling cable-car is a constant overhead.

At a grassy terrace populated by marmots and purple monkshood flowers, the path curves around a rock outcrop and large boulders, then widens and winds easily down across grass and dark earth to **Passo Pordoi** (2239m, **1hr**). ▸

> Accommodation includes the marvellous **Hotel Savoia** (tel 0462 601717, www.savoiahotel.net, credit cards accepted) with lovely original décor dating back to 1896.

Extension to the Ossario

From Passo Pordoi, a 30min stroll NE along a narrow road is the stark **Ossario**, a military memorial and mausoleum with the remains of over 8000 German and Austrian troops who lost their lives in the Dolomites during the two world wars.

Alongside Hotel Savoia, path n.601/AV2 begins a gentle ascent around Sass Beccè, past a chapel and romping marmots. Beyond rich gold carpets of globe flowers you look west to the majestic Catinaccio, and very soon to the Marmolada cradling its sprawling snowfield. A little further on, the way curves L past **Rifugio Fredarola** (2400m).

> **Rifugio Fredarola** (tel 0462 602072, www.fredarola.it, sleeps 32, open mid June to late Sept, credit cards accepted).

Now the Viel del Pan – a well-worn track wide enough for the mini-tractor used by the hut for transporting supplies – begins in earnest. It cuts E over slopes thick with an amazing wealth of wild blooms; black vanilla orchids and pasque flowers to mention but two. ▸ Not far along is a splendid natural podium for 'me and the Marmolada' snapshots, shortly before the stunningly positioned **Rifugio Viel del Pan** (2432m, **1hr**).

> **Rifugio Viel del Pan** (tel 339 3865241, info@rifugio vieldelpan.com, sleeps 24, open late June to late Sept). No dorm but lovely rooms. The crowds in summer attest to the quality of the cooking.

From the pass, SAD buses negotiate the hairpin bends to Val Badia and Val di Fassa.

Above are dark eroded volcanic cusps reminiscent of Easter Island statues.

Rifugio Viel del Pan, backed by curious lavic pinnacles

On the roadside is a cluster of eateries and a bus stop for the Dolomiti Bus to Malga Ciapela (Stage 6), as well as Trentino Trasporti to Val di Fassa.

A bit quieter now, the path continues below castle-like Sass Ciapel and the black lavic pinnacles Le Forfesc. Further along, ignore the fork L (to the Porta Vescovo cable-car) as the descent S begins. Slippery if wet, the path zigzags past a conifer or two before timber steps lead L around a rock face with several stretches of cable but minimal exposure. It quickly drops to the lakeside and **Rifugio Castiglioni** (2050m, 1hr 20min). ◀

Rifugio Castiglioni aka Marmolada (tel 0462 601681, **www.rifugiomarmolada.it**, sleeps 25 in dorm and rooms, open spring to autumn, credit cards accepted). A wonderful historic establishment with cosy sleeping quarters, helpful staff and a dining room that gazes at the Marmolada.

The **Lago di Fedaia dam** was constructed in 1956; it is 55m high, 342m long and holds 17 million cubic metres of water, and serves the hydro-electric power station at Malga Ciapela. Film buffs will recognise the dam wall from the *The Italian Job*!

STAGE 6
Rifugio Castiglioni to Passo San Pellegrino

Start	Rifugio Castiglioni
Distance	22km
Total ascent	1110m
Total descent	1240m
Grade	2
Time	7hr (can be shortened by 1hr 45min if you take the bus from the start to Malga Ciapela)
Note	The climber's variant across the Marmolada is not described here, as ice equipment and experience are essential. For info and guides, contact Rifugio Castiglioni.

An awfully long day but with plenty of variants in store. After the not especially exciting descent to Malga Ciapela (coverable by bus if desired), a rewarding traverse awaits. It entails 1000+m uphill, mostly on a 1915–18 military track for mules and men, with great views of the imposing 'back' side of the Marmolada and a host of outstanding Dolomites. Then a beautiful pasture valley lined with old photogenic hay barns leads on to Passo San Pellegrino, where the stage staggers to a comfortable end.

However, a worthwhile option is to make this a semi-rest day: stop over at Malga Ciapela and treat yourself to an exhilarating ride on the three-stage cable-car to discover the breathtaking glaciated Marmolada. From the second station at 2950m you can visit the poignant WW1 museum and explore Punta Serauta, perforated with wartime tunnels; then continue to the uppermost station – 3265m Punta Rocca – for spectacular 360-degree photo opportunities.

Between Rifugio Castiglioni and Malga Ciapela, maps show the AV2 following the road; however, savvy walkers proceed as follows:

From **Rifugio Castiglioni** (2050m), cross the dam wall and turn L (SE) along the peaceful traffic-free road above **Lago di Fedaia** (the name a reference to grazing). A second dam wall and small lake are passed on the way

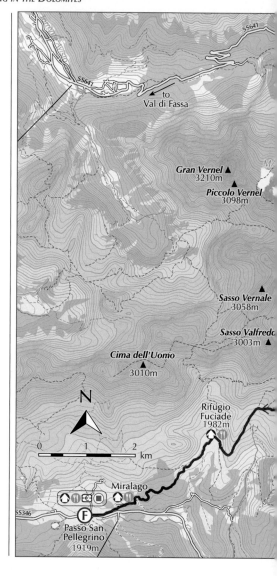

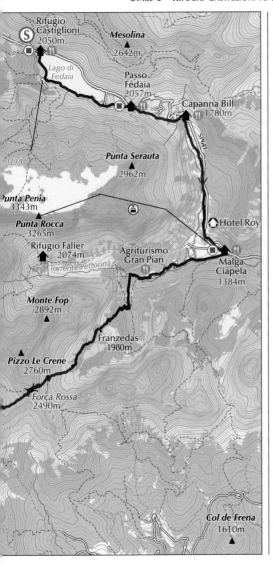

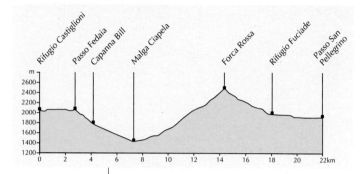

to a roadside bus stop and Passo Fedaia (2057m) with **Rifugio Passo Fedaia**.

> **Rifugio Passo Fedaia** (tel 0437 722007, www. rifugiofedaia.com, sleeps 25 (dorm and rooms), open mid June to mid Sept, credit cards accepted).

On the R side of the road, plunge down Pian di Lobia on a grassed ski slope (ESE), following a faint path. This curves under a chair lift and crosses a stream, continuing past the 1780m guesthouse **Capanna Bill**.

> **Capanna Bill** (tel 0437 722100, www.capannabill. com, open June to Sept).

Parallel to the road, continue S down to the end of the chair lift for a series of tracks and past a ski lift through a beautiful wood to **Hotel Roy**. It's not far down the road to the Marmolada cable-car and the handful of hotels that make up the resort of **Malga Ciapela** (1384m, **1hr 40min**). Cafés and restaurants. Do any grocery shopping here, as there are no further chances without detouring off-route.

> **Hotel Tyrolia** (tel 0437 522999, www.tyroliahotel. com, credit cards accepted) is good value.

THE MARMOLADA

The south face of the Marmolada can be admired en route to Forca Rossa

'Imagine a very thick slice of melon laid upon its side, and you will have a good bird's-eye notion of ... the Marmolata ... or else you might think of a vast dead tooth stopped up with snow.' – Botanist Reginald Farrer's delightful 1913 description.

The 'Queen of the Dolomites' stands 3342m high and 5km long. The earliest known summit attempt was in 1804 when a priest, a doctor and a lawyer set out to examine the glimmering ice sheet and put an end to superstitious beliefs. However, it was not until 1864 that Punta Penia, the highest elevation, was conquered by Austrian mountaineer Paul Grohmann and the Dimai brothers, his guides from Cortina.

The age of the glacier is unknown. Rapidly shrinking, it has lost 80% of its volume over the last century and is destined to disappear in 25–30 years. However, according to legend it was once lush and verdant pasture: one summer evening a lone old peasant stayed back to rake in her hay, as the weather appeared to be turning bad. Heedless of the admonitions from her companions, who were making for the valley to pay homage to the Virgin and invoke protection for the coming year, she pressed on with her labour. In next to no time she was caught up in a dramatic snow storm – sent as divine punishment. Alas, the weight of the deadly white cloak spelled her end, while the pastures hardened into the icy mass glacier that sprawls over the slope today.

She has not been alone in her icy tomb. The demarcation line between Italy and the former Hapsburg Empire ran the length of the crest and World War 1 soldiers perished on the treacherous high-altitude terrain of the Marmolada – the Austrians alone lost 300 men in a single avalanche in December 1916. To shelter their troops, they excavated the ingenious 'City of Ice', an astounding 12km network of tunnels through the glacier's eerie recesses. Survivors told of the uncanny pale-blue light, then the spine-chilling creaks and groans of the ice grinding over rock; however, they all appreciated the protection it gave them.

Opposite the cable-car, by all means cut across the meadows down to join the narrow road – go R through the camping ground.

◄ A matter of minutes downhill at Albergo Malga Ciapela, turn R on the narrow road that follows Torrente Pettorina WSW through a camping ground. With short-cuts it gains height in conifer woods thick with columbines and orchids and cows grazing in clearings, oblivious of the dramatic south wall of the Marmolada above. Past farm/restaurant **Agriturismo Gran Pian** is a bridge (1540m) – as per AV2 signs, stick to the rough jeep track, soon veering due S. Ignore turn-offs for Rifugio Falier and wind SW in steady ascent through wood.

The undergrowth is mostly larch, delicate pink alpenrose and bilberry shrubs, while overhead is triangular Monte Fop and Monte La Banca.

As the track dog-legs L towards the scatter of summer farms that is **Franzedas** (1980m), AV2 forks R on a signed path, whose WW1 military origin is soon obvious thanks to a gentle gradient and stone edging. ◄ The red earth fault where you are heading is clearly in view now, albeit still a fair way off. Keep plodding on amid bursts of bright wildflowers on the pale limestone and dark earth.

At last, on the lower edge of Pizzo Le Crene, and easily recognisable for the black cloud of chattering alpine choughs hanging over it, is **Forca Rossa** (2490m, **3hr 20min**), of strategic WW1 importance for supplying the Marmolada front. Malga Ciapela can be seen in the valley, now more than 1000m below! Once you've got your breath back, check out the panorama: due south, the jagged Focobon peaks stand out – encountered first-hand in the next stage – while close at hand west is a relic rock glacier below the Formenton-Sasso Valfredda barrier.

The descent paths are not always clear. The best advice is to follow signs for Fuchiade.

Drop down the path SW (and ignore the fork R) across red clay terrain and grass. It veers W via two distinct pasture basins enjoyed by horses and marmots. After a grassy ridge, AV2 curves NW for the short drop to the foot of a vast scree basin and immaculately kept meadows popular with families. Here stands **Rifugio Fuciade** (1982m).

Rifugio Fuciade (tel 0462 574281, www.fuciade.it, credit cards accepted). An upmarket guesthouse/restaurant.

Now a traffic-free lane (n.607) makes its leisurely way SW past a string of photogenic hay barns and chalets and into light woods, to **Albergo Miralago**.

Albergo Miralago (tel 0462 573088, www.albergomiralago.com, open June to Oct, credit cards accepted, good food).

Only 5min away is the road and **Passo San Pellegrino** (1919m, **2hr**), its namesake a sadly ramshackle hostel dating back to the 1400s for merchants and pilgrims en route to Venice and embarkation for the Holy Land. ▸

Various hotels, such as **Costabella** (tel 0462 573326, www.costabella.it, credit cards accepted).

There's an ATM here, and Trentino Trasporti buses to Moena in Val di Fassa thence Trento, or an occasional Dolomiti Bus runs to Falcade and beyond.

It's a lovely stroll down to Passo San Pellegrino

STAGE 7
Passo San Pellegrino to Rifugio Mulaz

Start	Passo San Pellegrino
Distance	13km
Total ascent	1040m
Total descent	380m
Grade	3
Time	5hr 30min – can be shortened by 50min using the cable-car at stage start

This is quite a full-on stage, passing through a brilliant range of scenery. It begins with a straightforward, if not exceptionally thrilling, traverse to Passo Valles, which hosts a great value refuge-cum-guesthouse – a perfect place to take a well-deserved break. If desired, this opening section can be shortened by 50min by taking the cable-car from Passo San Pellegrino to Col Margherita then the clear path SE to Forcella di Pradazzo.

Once through Passo Valles a spectacular section is revealed as the trek enters the realms of the awesome Pale di San Martino – one of the most rugged Dolomite ranges. It boasts soaring elegant *campanile* towers around a vast *altopiano*; an authentic lunar upland, its highest summit the 3192m Cima Vezzena. All is well protected under the auspices of a *parco naturale*. The ensuing three stages are spent within its borders on an exciting roller-coaster of sights and paths. However, this is not suitable terrain for beginners – and in fact the stretch as far as Rifugio Mulaz, with exposed and aided passages, verges on quite difficult.

From **Passo San Pellegrino** (1919m), opposite the former hostel, turn through the main car park following path n.658 signposted for Passo Valles. It strikes out SE across marshy terrain chopped up by the hoofs of cows and horses. You quickly enter a pretty wood with larch and juniper and cross a cascading stream. Passing under the Col Margherita cable-car, the climb continues steadily SE.

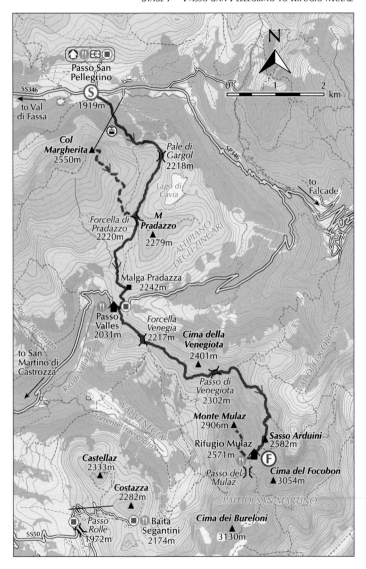

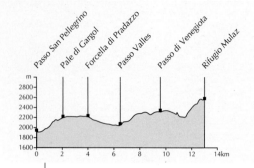

As a ski slope is reached, turn uphill for 200 metres and look for a small marked path L into the trees. Follow this up across another piste to signposts close to a tarn. Here continue steeply uphill through trees and rocks to the col **Pale di Gargol** aka Forcella Cargol (2218m). You're now on the edge of the Altipiano degli Zingari, a gently sloping upland scattered with boulders.

Follow cairns and red/white waymarks mostly SW, meandering amid flowers and rocky terrain to **Forcella di Pradazzo** (2220m, **1hr 45min**), where the route from the Col Margherita cable-car joins up. Head S down the dirt track beneath Monte Pradazzo, cutting corners. Accompanied by clanging cow bells, you have time to admire the spread of the vast slabs of the metamorphic Lagorai chain extending east–north.

To exit here, catch the weekend-only summer bus to Falcade (Dolomiti Bus) or Val di Fassa (Trentino Trasporti).

After **Malga Pradazzo** (2242m) it's not far to Passo Valles (2031m, **30min**) and the excellent family-run **Rifugio Passo Valles**. ◄

Rifugio Passo Valles (tel 0437 599136, www.passovalles.com, sleeps 40, open mid June to mid Oct, credit cards accepted). Of the superb meals to be enjoyed here, don't miss *gnocchi con ricotta affumicata* (delicate potato dumplings with smoked cheese). An adorable ageing St Bernard dog may be in residence.

Across the road near the chapel, take path n.751 as it climbs S, zigzagging to the R of a sharp ridge, traversing impressive grey-cream striations. Bearing SE over dark terrain that is well grassed and flowered, the path ascends easily below Cima Valles to a crest and the notch of **Forcella Venegia** (2217m). ▶

The path proceeds ESE along the grassy crest past a tiny lake and grazing sheep, dipping briefly S to avoid Cima della Venegiota. With good chances of spotting marmots, it's not far to **Passo di Venegiota** (2302m, **1hr 15min**).

Now on the northern side of Monte Mulaz, you cross crumbly terrain accompanied by the first of a series of short but reassuring cables. A grassy shoulder opens onto

The magnificent Cimon della Pala (south-southeast), dubbed the 'Matterhorn of the Dolomites', lords it over deep Val Venegia; beyond stretches the Lagorai chain.

An aided passage on the way to Rifugio Mulaz

Ascending below Sasso Arduini, with a view to Falcade

a lengthy scree descent SE above a rock-strewn basin, while ahead the elegant Focobon peaks come into view a little at a time.

A short, sheer cliff is rounded thanks to an aided section as AV2 moves S into upper Val di Focobon. Climbing steadily, you fork L up a rusty red gully equipped with long stretches of cable. Watch out for falling stones here. You emerge for a brief respite on a grassy flat but soon resume S, following paint splashes and cables up pale rock slabs.

The name Focobon may derive from buon fuoco, or 'fire', referring to the reddish reflected sun's rays caught by the peaks.

A near-vertical section concludes at a col amid myriad wildflowers for the short detour to 2582m **Sasso Arduini**, a wonderful belvedere named after a president of the Venice CAI branch which constructed the nearby refuge. This is also a magnificent viewpoint for the fantastic Focobon peaks and their remnant hanging glacier. ◀

A short path drops to the spectacularly positioned **Rifugio Mulaz** (2571m, **2hr**).

Rifugio Mulaz (tel 0437 599420 or 338 5924343, rifugiomulaz@gmail.com, CAI, sleeps 52, open mid June to end Sept). They do a hearty *minestrone*, and the delicious *pasta con ragù* comes in mountainous

servings. State-of-the-art technology powers the refuge.

Rifugio Mulaz in its stony setting

The hut's full name is Rifugio Giuseppe Volpi al Mulaz, for the Venetian entrepreneur who launched the city's mainland industrial development in the 1910s – a questionable merit – along with the world-famous film festival. 'Mulaz', on the other hand, is probably related to 'mule' for the shape of the adjacent mountain.

Side trip to Monte Mulaz (1hr 20min return)

If you have energy to burn, from the refuge's rocky plat-form take the well-marked path climbing NNW to the panoramic summit of 2906m **Monte Mulaz**.

Exit route

An exit route is feasible by way of path n.710 via nearby **Passo del Mulaz**. The way descends into upper Val Venegia before heading uphill to Baita Segantini (2hr 10min) for a bus or chair lift to Passo Rolle. From there, Trentino Trasporti buses continue to San Martino di Castrozza and Feltre.

STAGE 8
Rifugio Mulaz to Rifugio Rosetta

Start	Rifugio Mulaz
Distance	7.5km
Total ascent	750m
Total descent	740m
Grade	3+
Time	4hr 15min

This massively rewarding and extremely tiring stage takes AV2 walkers via rugged passages into the breathtaking heart of the Pale di San Martino *altipiano*, where humans are but minuscule dots on an immense limestone upland that extends for over 50km². It was smoothed by bodies of ice 10,000 years ago and subsequently eroded into a karst rockscape. In these desolate surrounds, brilliant alpine flowers miraculously thrive on thin layers of soil detritus blown in by the wind.

A good head for heights and a sure foot are essential, along with good stable weather. Early summer walkers may need an ice axe and crampons to deal with hard snow – if in doubt, enquire of the Rifugio Mulaz guardian before setting out.

First off is a short traverse and dizzy aided climb to Passo delle Farangole on a well-maintained path. A vertical gully is then negotiated in descent with the help of cables and rungs. A path continues for a marvellous, lengthy panoramic traverse – the 'Sentiero delle Farangole' – high over Val delle Comelle, dwelling place of nymphs capable of whisking away a man's reason. Once Pian dei Cantoni is reached, all that remains is a steady ascent over the lunar landscape to a comfortable *rifugio*. Take care on this final stretch, as orientation can be a problem in the mist which can roll in at the drop of a hat even on a bright sunny day, obscuring useful landmarks.

If the exposure and aided stretches don't sound like your cup of tea, bail out on the exit route given in Stage 7.

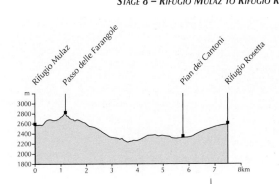

From **Rifugio Mulaz** (2571m), go uphill on path n.703, which soon forks L to zigzag up a path reinforced with tree trunks to the notch of **Forcella Margherita** (2655m). Now beneath soaring Cima del Focobon, the path traverses a vast scree basin where snow lingers, before heading E, ever steeper, towards that deep cut between two *campanile* towers. Steel staples and lengths of cable help on the scramble up to **Passo delle Farangole** (2814m, **1hr 15min**) – a dizzy perch, its apt name meaning 'deep incision'.

Passo delle Farangole, squeezed between rock towers

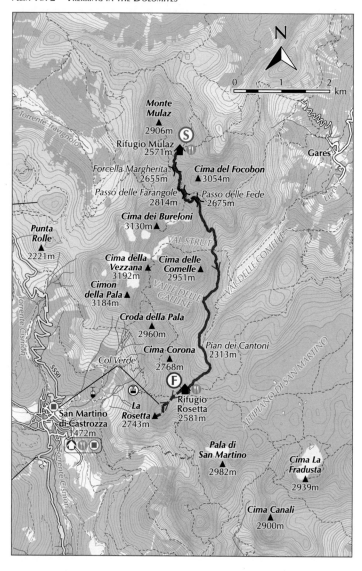

▶ The ensuing plunge sticks close to the L side of this vertical chimney with lengths of cable all the way down, concluding with rungs and a ladder. At the bottom keep L on easier – if mobile – scree, where fleet-hoofed chamois are at home. Down into a basin of broken rock, curve R past **Passo delle Fede** (2675m), a reference to the sheep that once grazed up here.

Bearing S over Val Grande, drop steadily over flowered grassy terrain at the foot of soaring peaks. The undulating Altipiano di San Martino spreads out southeast, while hundreds of metres below is the dramatic trough of sheer sided Val delle Comelle. Ignore

Take special care on the next section not to dislodge stones, which could endanger other walkers.

Descending from Passo delle Farangole

the 2290m fork R for Valstrut and 3192m Cima della Vezzana, the highest in the San Martino group and a magnet for mountaineers.

The path can feel a little exposed and vertiginous as it cuts across sheer mountainsides. After a grassy shoulder studded with edelweiss and alpine thrift, it begins to climb once more, overshadowed by Cima delle Comelle.

Long aided stretches cross rock faces before a shallow chasm and a narrow chimney at the foot of **Valle delle Galline** ('valley of chickens'!). At last a broad pasture corner dotted with boulders is gained and there are satisfying views back over the path covered. Phew!

A gentle gradient sees you dip into a marvellous basin with blinding white rivers of scree carpeted with yellow poppies that fill the air with their fragrance. This is **Pian dei Cantoni** (2313m, **2hr 15min**). Joined by a path from Gares, n.703 begins the final climb for the day. Marked by the odd red/white paint splash and cairns, it makes its way up to the plateau pitted with a surprising number of limestone dolina depressions, filled either with snow or tiny baby gentians.

At a signed junction, AV2 joins an old military track that is in remarkably good condition, and at the very last minute sees and gains the comfortable **Rifugio Rosetta** (2581m, **45min**).

> **Rifugio Rosetta** aka Giovanni Pedrotti (tel 0439 68308, **www.rifugiorosetta.it**, CAI-SAT, sleeps 80, open mid June to late Sept, credit cards accepted). Generous portions of dishes such as flavoursome *canederli* (dumplings) are served in the bustling dining room.
>
> The spacious refuge dates to 1890. However, it was burnt down in both world wars, to be rebuilt and since enlarged by SAT, the Trento branch of the Italian Alpine Club, who named it after a past president. Luckily, recent renovation has not robbed it of its old alpine-style charm in the dorms and timber hallways.

Rifugio Rosetta

On a clear day, do find the time for the easy side trip to La Rosetta.

Side trip to La Rosetta (1hr return)

▶ From the refuge, follow the path SW towards the cable-car, then turn off up the vast incline to the 2743m **La Rosetta** 'pulpit' summit and cross for heart-stopping views down over the township of San Martino di Castrozza and beyond to the metamorphic Lagorai chain and even the glaciated Ortles-Cevedale groups in the distance. Closer at hand are Croda della Pala (north) and Cimon della Pala (north-northwest), although the highest of the group, Cima Vezzana, is partially concealed to the north.

'Rosetta' is the delicate pinkish hue the mountain assumes with the first rays of morning sun.

Exit route

Rifugio Rosetta is a convenient place to leave (if you must) – or join – AV2, thanks to the nearby cable-car to Col Verde, thence gondola lift and shuttle bus to the chic alpine resort of San Martino di Castrozza. Or, on foot, there's the exhilarating path n.701 – allow 1hr 30min to Col Verde, and the same again to San Martino. ▶

Tourist office (tel 0439 768867), hotels, Trentino Trasporti coach runs via Fiera di Primiero to Feltre for trains.

STAGE 9
Rifugio Rosetta to Rifugio Treviso

Start	Rifugio Rosetta
Distance	13km
Total ascent	790m
Total descent	1740m
Grade	3
Time	6hr 15min

The stage begins by following a leisurely mule track with lots of zigzags and a gentle gradient. However, be aware that next comes a long, aided stretch, which is exciting but quite exposed – not everyone's cup of tea. A magnificent traverse ensues to the excellent Rifugio Pradidali before another difficult (but shorter) passage leading up to Passo delle Lede. Then comes a winding descent that touches on a beautifully placed unmanned bivouac hut. A final climb and it all comes to a happy conclusion at a refuge in the welcoming cover of woods in magnificent Val Canali – another of the wonders of the Pale di San Martino.

The airy section after Rifugio Pradidali can easily be avoided thanks to a lovely lower path that loops through Val Canali – described below. Dropping almost 1000m before a climb of 300m, it is half an hour quicker.

After the rigours of yesterday, you may like to make this a semi-rest day and split the stage by overnighting at the hospitable Rifugio Pradidali, giving yourself time to fully enjoy the superb landscapes.

The bleached mountainsides contrast strongly with the dark, almost luscious, green of the forested valleys far below, while the rock faces harbour saxifrages, thrift and the divine endemic, Moretti's bellflower.

From **Rifugio Rosetta** (2581m), turn R (S) on the broad stony track n.702 and continue via **Passo di Val Roda** (2572m) before dropping to skirt the base of Croda di Roda. ◄

There's a curious story behind the unusual **mule track** followed on the opening stretch. Leaving the outskirts of San Martino to climb Val di Roda to the plateau – a total ascent of 1000m (tunnel included) – it was the brainchild of Leipzig native Baron von Lesser. He funded it with lotteries and donations

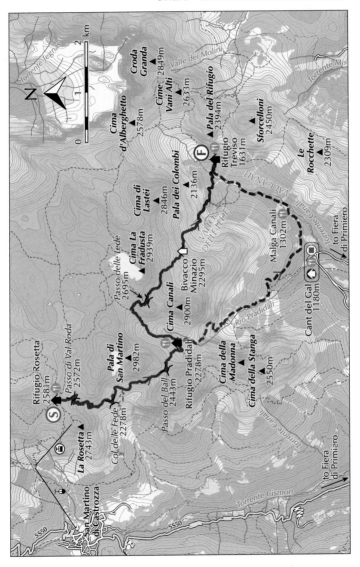

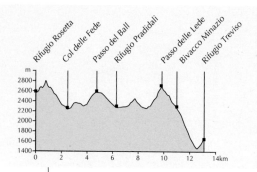

from 1905–12, under the Hapsburg Empire. As the story goes, workers were paid by the metre rather than on a time basis and ingeniously stretched out the track – judging by its interminable zigzags (240 in total) and all but imperceptible gradient! In another version the gentle gradient was intentional so as to ensure a smooth ride on horseback for the baron's disabled daughter.

Eventually, 300m lower, you veer L (E) along man-made ledges rounding **Col delle Fede** (2278m), a grassed outcrop studded with edelweiss. A level stretch leads across a scree valley flanking the impressive Pala di San Martino. Not far on, AV2 leaves the old mule track (which continues its crazy zigzagging descent), breaking off SSE on n.715 and sticking to the L flank of a desolate snow-streaked valley.

Soon, following a sign recommending inexperienced walkers rope up and use karabiners, is the beginning of a guiding cable anchored to the rock as you edge along narrow ledges and clamber hands-on up rock faces. Tackle this with appropriate care – the going can be pretty giddy as well as extremely beautiful.

A path reappears for the final clamber to **Passo del Ball** (2443m, **2hr**). ◄ A dramatic opening between Cima di Ball and Cima Pradidali, it grants your first view of the awesome Cima Canali to the east, while the impressive

Passo del Ball was named in honour of John Ball, one of the initiators of Dolomite mountaineering and first president of the Alpine Club in England.

A long aided stretch climbs to Passo del Ball

Sass Maor stands out to the south, with the Vette Feltrine beyond.

It's an easy descent E, dodging toppled boulders and scree to reach **Rifugio Pradidali** (2278m, **25min**).

Rifugio Pradidali (tel 0439 64180 or 348 2455732, **www.rifugiopradidali.com**, CAI, sleeps 64, open mid June to late Sept). This modern establishment replaces the historic timber-panelled Pravitali Hütte erected back in 1896 by the Dresden Alpine Club. Run by a knowledgeable alpine guide, it is a welcoming place and has a dining room with huge glass windows. The name may derive from the *prati gialli* (yellow meadows) down in the valley, possibly for the profusion of poppies.

For walkers who would prefer to avoid the steep crossing of Passo delle Lede – or bail out here – an easier variant is given.

Variant to Rifugio Treviso (3hr 15min)

From Rifugio Pradidali (2278m), descend S on path n.709, zigzagging down the head of **Val Pradidali** on steep stretches aided by guiding cables. Lower down are easier gradients and pine forest. After 1hr 30min in descent, turn L as per signposting for Malga Canali and Rifugio Treviso (unless you'd prefer to drop a further 30min to 1180m and two restaurant-guesthouses, La Ritonda (tel 0439 762223) and Cant del Gal (tel 0439 62997, www.cantdelgal.it). ◄ A delightful undulating path through shady wood leads around NE via farm-eatery Malga Canali (1302m) in a lovely setting. Beyond a car park, track n.707 leads N up Val Canali to cross the watercourse R and start the climb E, joined by the main AV2 route for **Rifugio Treviso**.

Trentino Trasporti bus to Fiera di Primiero.

When you can drag yourself away from the comforts of Rifugio Pradidali, head N up the immense valley on n.709 in the shadow of towering Cima Canali and Cima Wilma. A clear path across smashed rock leads around Lago Pradidali, usually silted up late summer but sporting a pretty green hue earlier in the season. After an outcrop, bear R, gaining considerable height via a series of terraces.

Some 40min up is a signed junction where n.711/AV2 forks R (NE). Inexperienced walkers are advised to rope up and use karabiners now as cables lead up a moderately exposed rock face flanking a gully. Up at a detritus terrace you can relax and drink in the amazing views as far as the Marmolada.

Now keep your eyes peeled for red paint marks, heading E for the most part, with several easy hands-on bits but no exposure. The reward is **Passo delle Lede** (2695m, **1hr 30min**) – what a spot! The Pala di San Martino and partner Cima Immink steal the show to the west, while to the east La Fradusta does its best to impress. The eastern side of the pass is quite different; desolate Vallon delle Lede is wilder and apparently only visited by AV2 walkers.

A good path drops SE across scree towards flowered patches and pasture enjoyed by sheep, and in view of the scattered debris of a US plane that crashed here in 1957. Coming into sight at the very last minute is sturdy wooden hut **Bivacco Minazio** (2295m, **50min**) (bunk beds and blankets for 12, water nearby). ▶

Intending users will need their own stove and utensils.

Rifugio Treviso (the day's destination) can be spotted ensconced in trees on the opposite side of Val Canali – not to mention the rugged crest with tomorrow's route.

In relentless descent, the path snakes down the valley middle with short hands-on rock faces. At the 2000m mark, springy dwarf mountain pine and spruce appear. Further down you veer L across a bleached stream bed below Pala dei Colombi, where loose stones underfoot and increased steepness make for tiring going.

At Bivacco Minazio (photo: Martin Price)

R at the fork is an exit route to Cant del Gal (30min) and bus stop.

Shady beech wood is quite enjoyable after days on end of rockscapes, and birdsong is a lovely accompaniment. Keeping L at a fork, a soft path leads to a bridge (1450m) over a gushing river, although a stream soon needs to be leapt over. ◄

Now gird your loins for the last 25min leg in gentle ascent through woods and past waterfalls, to **Rifugio Treviso** (1631m, **1hr 30min**).

Rifugio Treviso (tel 0439 62311, rifugiotreviso@ gmail.com, CAI, sleeps 44, open late June to end Sept, credit cards accepted). Named for the CAI branch that owns it, this hospitable place is run by a knowledgeable alpine guide. It has undergone extensive modernisation and boasts lovely bathrooms, while retaining its comfortable dining room and old fireplace, as well as creaky timber floors and old-style sleeping cubicles. Power comes from the turbine connected with the nearby waterfall. This is a VIP base for climbers who easily outnumber AV2 walkers, as it is said that Val Canali boasts the best limestone in the whole of the Dolomites. Many visitors come for the food: the *minestrone* is especially delicious, while an unusual dish is *carne salada con fagioli*, thinly sliced cured beef seasoned with lemon and served with brown beans.

STAGE 10
Rifugio Treviso to Passo Cereda

Start	Rifugio Treviso
Distance	8.5km
Total ascent	750m
Total descent	1010m
Grade	2–3
Time	4hr 30min

A very enjoyable stroll through cool forest opens this stage, before a steepish climb to a strategic col. Here AV2 bids farewell to the spectacular Pale di San Martino as vistas open onto the Cimònega and Vette Feltrine chains, where the route spends its concluding days. In the meantime a couple of hours are spent on the equivalent of a partly exposed goat's path skirting crumbling gullies and steep slopes where overhangs are festooned with colourful blooms. A sure foot is essential. The sounds of 'civilisation' waft up from farming communities far below: wood chopping, dogs barking, cows mooing. The day wraps up with a knee-testing descent to meadows and a rural road pass where comfortable refuge-hotels await. Here, buses are on hand for walkers who decide to call it a day so as to avoid the challenging wild paths ahead on the final three stages.

On the other hand, should you not feel up to this strenuous crossing, you could exit AV2 by following the route as far as the Campigol d'Oltro junction and then fork R in descent to Val Canali thence Cant del Gal (2hr) – see the variant in Stage 9 for local info.

Turn L out of the front door of **Rifugio Treviso** (1631m) and along the side wall with its sundial. Heading S, path n.718 crosses the first of three boulder-choked gullies. In beech and pine forest pretty with purple orchids, it continues mostly on a level to the **Campigol d'Oltro** junction (1730m). Here, AV2 forks L (SE) to start the ascent.

Shrubs and dwarf mountain pines give way to larch and alpenrose then stones and sparse grass on this

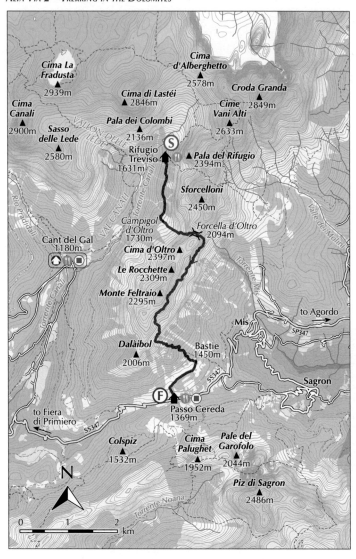

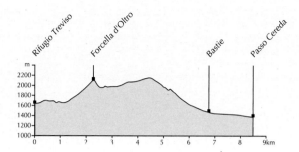

relentless but straightforward climb. Higher up, the path moves to the L of the valley to avoid snow tongues. Make the most of getting-your-breath-back pauses to admire the elegant Sass Maor (due west) and the Vallon delle Lede visited yesterday.

Forcella d'Oltro (2094m, **1hr 40min**) is distinguished by a pointed rock sentinel. It affords a vast outlook over rolling woodland and meadows – quite a contrast to the last few days! ▶

From here on, expect to see spectacular clumps of endemic Moretti's bellflower sheltering in overhangs.

The long traverse after Forcella d'Oltro

Far below nestles the farming village of Gosaldo.

Watch your step, as the path immediately drops steeply on loose stones, bearing R to begin its long traverse SW. On grassy earth and rock terrain, the going is quite narrow and exposed in spots. It skirts sheer flanks below Cima d'Oltro then Le Rocchette. ◄

After passing Monte Feltraio you climb a little, back to the 2000m mark, where bizarre stone pinnacles stick out of the mountainsides. Brace your knees as an abrupt veer L marks the start of a plunging descent as the path weaves its way SE through what resembles a petrified forest interspersed with live conifers. Watch your step on the loose stones.

Further down is cooler woodland where the gradient eases and beech leaves and pine needles make for softer going underfoot. You finally emerge on a narrow surfaced road at 1450m (**Bastie**) and a radio mast. Turn R (SW) for a leisurely stroll past meadows with barns in a pastoral setting.

Trentino Trasporti buses run to Fiera di Primiero for connections to Feltre and trains. Dolomiti Bus service runs to Agordo and on to Belluno for the railway.

As you approach the pass, leave the road on an unmarked path L via a derelict building; this brings you out alongside **Rifugio Passo Cereda** (1369m, **2hr 50min**), looking over to the light grey rock points of Pale del Garofolo. ◄

Accommodation and memorable meals are available at **Rifugio Passo Cereda** (tel 0439 65030, **www.rifugiocereda.com**, sleeps 65 (rooms and dorm), open May to Oct, credit cards accepted) or at nearby **Agritur Broch** (tel 0439 65028, **www. agriturismobroch.it**, sleeps 16 (rooms and dorm), open June–Oct, credit cards accepted).

STAGE 11
Passo Cereda to Rifugio Boz

Start	Passo Cereda
Distance	13.5km
Total ascent	1250m
Total descent	900m
Grade	3
Time	7hr

Today the trek makes its way across the Cimònega group to enter the Parco Nazionale delle Dolomiti Bellunesi, a region of great wild natural beauty, brilliant endemic flora – and very few walkers. Rugged, exciting days lie ahead. This long stage is both non-stop awesome and decidedly demanding. The ascent to Passo del Comedon is challenging and should not be embarked upon in anything but good weather. The terrain is unstable and the top section subject to erosion, as it gets progressively eaten away by heavy rain. The good news is that it has been reinforced with timber planks, making progress a little easier. Next comes a clear path through upper Val Canzoi, and a magnificent amphitheatre where Bivacco Feltre-Bodo stands – do consider an overnight stay if you can rustle up some food and cooking equipment beforehand, as it will make the follow-on all the more enjoyable.

The ensuing section is a narrow path cutting the flanks of Sass de Mura in a blaze of wildflowers. This long day comes to an end at the hospitable 'log cabin' Rifugio Boz, which excels at feeding ravenous AV2 walkers.

From **Passo Cereda** (1369m), take the narrow road opposite the *rifugio*. A batch of signposts (including n.801) point you gently uphill past a chapel. About 10min (750m) in, keep L for AV2/801, a lane heading E. Further along a signed path takes over, dropping through woodland and alongside meadows to join a lane near barns at **Casere** (1297m).

Turn R and stick with the lane as it crosses side streams, climbing gently, well above the village of Sagron

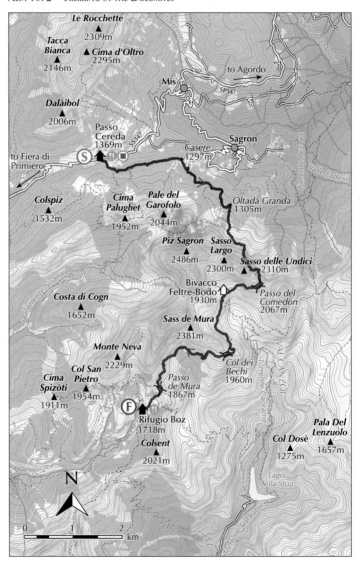

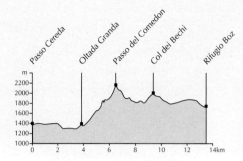

and hamlets. At the fork of **Oltada Granda** (1305m), take the well-marked path 801 which branches R up into the forest beneath Piz Sagron. This finally emerges from tree cover onto bleached broken rock to give superb views over farming hamlets backed by Monte Agner (north) and the Civetta (north-northeast), to name just two.

Accompanied by scattered larch and dwarf mountain pine, head mostly SSE beneath sheer rock walls before heading across a messy rubble gully for zigzags to a saddle under Sasso Largo. On this stretch quite a few lengths of cable attached to the cliffs are of help, while a sequence of oblique ledges make for pleasurable walking. ▶

After hugging the flanks of **Sasso delle Undici**, the way moves onto soft fine scree where wooden traverses anchor the terrain and aid progress up the eroded, near-vertical slope. It's with some relief that you clamber out at **Passo del Comedon** (2067m, **4hr**), an old smugglers' pass that now comes under the Parco Nazionale delle Dolomiti Bellunesi. ▶

The path turns R (W) and reaches a notch before descending a gully of shattered rock to the beautiful cirque where a carpet of edelweiss surrounds the two corrugated iron huts of **Bivacco Feltre-Bodo** (1930m, **30min**) (bunks and blankets for 19, water nearby). ▶

N.801 heads S downhill past lovely waterfalls and a fork (ignore n.806, which plunges to Val Canzoi). In a

At rest stops, check the rock faces for the exquisite devil's claw blooms.

At your feet to the south is the emerald-green Lago della Stua in Val Canzoi.

Piz Sagron dominates to the northwest, kept company by Sasso Largo and Sasso delle Undici.

99

Clambering up to Passo del Comedon

semi-circle over this spectacular upper valley, the path zigzags steeply and relentlessly up to **Col dei Bechi** (1960m) on a dizzy narrow ridge where chamois hang out. The rugged spine and peaks of the Vette Feltrine unfold ahead to the southwest – an inspiring sight.

This is the Troi dei Caserini, the 'way of the shepherds', who used it until recently. Narrow but clear, it heads W, hugging the stark rock face studded with wonderful flowers like endemic columbines. Reassuring cables accompany walkers along narrow ledges. Trickling cascades are crossed under the magnificent Sass de Mura.

Curving S high over the head of Val di Alvis, the concluding tract to the pass entails a couple more tricky passages. In the vicinity of wartime tunnels gouged out of the rock, the main grassy crest is gained, followed by the broad saddle of **Passo de Mura** (1867m, **2hr 15min**). ◀ Sharing a muddy path with the cows, head SW over pasture to **Rifugio Boz** (1718m, **15min**).

The modern-day boundary between the Trentino and Veneto regions, Passo de Mura once separated the Hapsburg Empire from the Kingdom of Italy – hence the vestiges of the military track.

Rifugio Boz (tel 0439 64448 or 340 9979332, **www.rifugioboz.it**, CAI, sleeps 34, open mid June to late Sept). The cosy dining room of this modest

Leaving Col dei Bechi

converted farm is warmed by a log fire. Local dairy products are served, such as *schiz* – a fresh local cheese that is pan-fried with cream.

The outlook is towards a curious bank of light grey rock with soaring bastions and striking parallel strata verging on the horizontal. These are the Vette Feltrine; traversed in their entirety tomorrow. Sweet dreams!

Exit route
From Rifugio Boz, take path n.727 downhill to join a stony track heading SW to Rifugio Fonteghi (**2hr**, tel 0439 67043, www.rifugiofonteghi.it, sleeps 18, open June to Oct). Thereafter, walk mostly W for 6km (**2hr**) on a surfaced road down the Val Noana gorge to the village of Imer (670m). ▶

Trentino Trasporti buses to Feltre.

STAGE 12
Rifugio Boz to Rifugio Dal Piaz

Start	Rifugio Boz
Distance	14km
Total ascent	940m
Total descent	670m
Grade	3
Time	6hr
Note	Carry plenty of drinking water

An exhilarating, awesome and unforgettable conclusion (almost) to the AV2, this stage is a drawn-out traverse of the wildly beautiful Vette Feltrine. A world unto themselves, this string of rugged peaks and contiguous valleys is safeguarded under the national park. Visitors are requested not to leave marked paths or gather plant or mineral specimens. Interest levels are high for flora and geology buffs, especially on today's last leg: finds have included fossil-rich *rosso ammonitico* rock with flint insets, along with fish teeth, sea urchins and myriad shells – Rifugio Dal Piaz has a marvellous display.

In terms of difficulty, one section stands out: Passo di Finestra to Sasso di Scarnia is no Sunday stroll. It is constantly exposed, necessitating a sure foot and no problems with vertigo. (Should this not appeal, take the exit route given at the end of Stage 11). Thereafter, the going is more straightforward, with a better path on easier terrain. Further on is Piazza del Diavolo; it is said the uncannily silent 'devil's square' used to be a favourite haunt of witches. These days it's quite safe thanks to the priest from nearby Vignui, who banished the practitioners of evil by planting a huge cross there.

A final 'but' concerns the mist that can rise unexpectedly from the adjoining plain, quickly shrouding the mountains and concealing landmarks. However, in good conditions the stage is extraordinarily scenic.

From **Rifugio Boz** (1718m) n.801/AV2 strikes out S, negotiating a muddy livestock path across the light wooded flanks of Colsent to reach **Passo di Finestra** (1766m, **40min**) – 'window pass' – where views open up towards the Veneto plain.

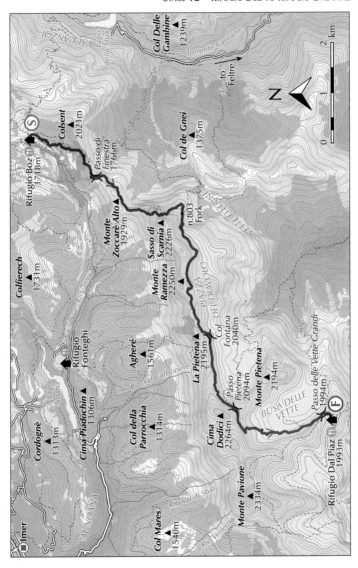

Watch your rucksack doesn't catch on the many overhangs.

Keep R (SW) now for a remarkable route, heritage of hunters and WW1 soldiers. Hewn into the rock face at times, narrow and exposed as it crosses eroded gullies, the path proceeds SW below **Monte Zoccarè Alto** through a veritable rock garden. Sprays of slender long-stemmed edelweiss alternate with milky saxifrage and dazzling-blue Moretti's bellflower, very much at home here. ◀

A tricky passage fitted with a reassuring stretch of hand cable is followed by an exposed narrow neck. Steps then zigzag upwards through bushy vegetation to more cable and another dizzy bridge passage where a clear head and sure foot are essential. Then what feels like a near-vertical goat's path leads up a spur to a 2060m shoulder at the base of soaring **Sasso di Scarnia** (**2hr**). The

Walkers dwarfed by Sasso di Scarnia

104

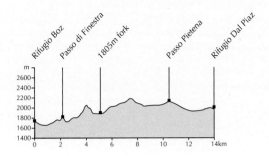

worst is behind you now as things improve a fair bit, but there's still a long way to go.

Through a maze of boulders, AV2 heads due S in descent with a few clambers but no exposure. The path resumes a W trend through dwarf mountain pines, passing a **1805m fork** (where n.803 turns off via Forcella di Scarnia for Vignui).

On a wider track you proceed in gentle ascent over a karstic landscape featuring dolina depressions, and into the vast Costa Alpe Ramezza amphitheatre. A marked curve across scree cuts the midriff of **Monte Ramezza**, and you gain a grassy crest (2050m) in the vicinity of an aerial – a rare landmark! From this angle the mountain's awesome face is revealed: infinite layers of creamy stone.

A brief narrow stretch on the N of the ridge concludes with a drop on a grassy slope facing Cima del Diavolo, as you head for Piazza del Diavolo to be dwarfed by flows of chaotic shattered rocks. Ignore a stone marked 'Giazzera' at a faint turn-off for a natural ice cave some 200m lower down – only explorable with appropriate equipment. ▸

After a lovely stretch past **Col Fontana** (2040m) is a stony-grassy bowl housing a ruined farm. Below Cima Dodici, bear SW over Busa di Pietena and its vast red slabs and curious piles of eroded rocks like giant's

Men from Pedavena used to trek up here to cut blocks from a gigantic frozen cone and carry them all the way down to the brewery (see Stage 13).

In autumn of 1944, Busa di Pietena was the base for 300 antifascist partisans with escaped British servicemen and the mountaineer Bill Tilman.

tiddlywinks. ◄ At **Passo Pietena** (2094m, **2hr 40min**) the bulk of Monte Pavione looms to the west.

The path curves S into magnificent Busa delle Vette, a veritable sea of karstic dolinas and grassed-over glacial mounds. Bells from the cows of the summer farm resound across the basin, which was once known as Busa delle Meraviglie ('cirque of wonders') for its wealth of natural marvels including bright blue delphiniums as well as hawks. You're joined by the farm jeep track for the gentle climb to **Passo delle Vette Grandi** (1994m). Only minutes down the other side, at last, is **Rifugio Dal Piaz** (1993m, **40min**).

> **Rifugio Dal Piaz** (tel 0439 9065, www.rifugio dalpiaz.com, CAI, sleeps 22, open mid June to late Sept). Named after a prominent geologist, the hut specialises in soups and polenta with melted cheese or stewed beef.

The stage end on the edge of the Vette Feltrine means vast views

The outlook here is definitely non-dolomitic but wonderful all the same. There are vast views across the Piave river plain and even to the Adriatic coast on a clear day. After dark, the lowlands fill up with the twinkling lights of 'civilisation' – your destination tomorrow.

STAGE 13
Rifugio Dal Piaz to Feltre

Start	Rifugio Dal Piaz
Distance	19km
Total ascent	Negligible
Total descent	1820m
Grade	2
Time	4hr 30min (shortened to 1hr 30min by exiting at Passo Croce d'Aune)

As the memorable AV2 draws to its conclusion, vast views and wildflowers add to the fascination today. A leisurely descent on a lane is followed by paths through shady woodland, dropping via mountainside hamlets with traditional farm buildings. Further down in the valley the Pedavena brewery and its gardens await, as do creature comforts and ongoing transport at the attractive Renaissance town of Feltre, where the AV2 comes to an end, like all good things must!

In view of the lengthy descent (the final 9.5km of which is on surfaced roads, albeit minor) you may prefer to call it a day at the Croce d'Aune road pass, where café-restaurants and accommodation are available, not to mention a bus (or taxi) to Pedavena and Feltre.

From **Rifugio Dal Piaz** (1993m) n.801 cuts S down grassed flanks onto an old military lane that snakes its way down these impervious mountainsides with tight corners and plenty of shortcuts. ▶ Great views can be enjoyed back to the Vette Feltrine atop imposing cliff barriers.

After **Col dei Cavai** (1472m), a rough and tiring stony stretch plunges through wood, where mud can mean slippery going after rain. You end up at a signed **path junction** (1054m, **1hr 30min**) near a water trough and the start of a minor surfaced road.

Rock faces host colonies of bear's-ear primrose and saxifrage rosettes, while meadows are thick with pheasant's-eye narcissus.

Exit route to Passo Croce d'Aune (5min)
Follow the road straight ahead past houses for the brief distance to **Passo Croce d'Aune** (1015m). Here you'll find

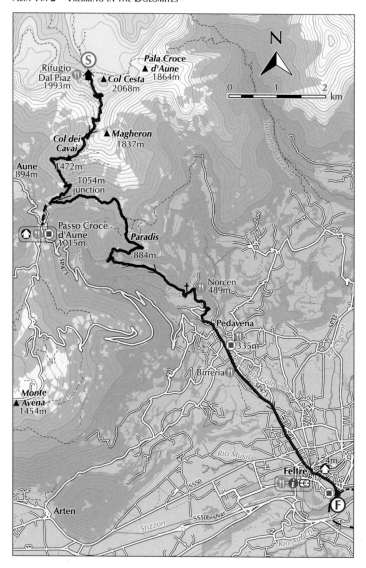

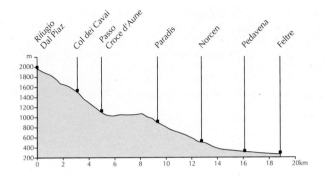

two hotel-restaurants – Albergo Croce d'Aune (tel 0439 977000, https://albergocrocedaune.it) and Al Camoscio (tel 0439 977058) – as well as a Parco Nazionale delle Dolomiti Bellunesi info point, and of great importance a bus stop for the summertime Dolomiti Bus run via Pedavena to Feltre (except Sundays and public holidays). Or you can call a taxi (tel 329 2255610).

At the 1054m path junction, n.801/AV2 forks L on a stony lane for a mostly level stroll E through beautiful shady beech and conifer forest. ▶ Just under 2km along, you're pointed R onto a path in descent.

The way continues down through trees essentially SE, touching on ruined stone huts and a clearing or two. Signage is regular and the route is clear. After crossing a lane, you pass a wooden crucifix and continue down to emerge at **Paradis** (884m, **45min**) – a beautiful pasture

This stretch is believed to follow the ancient Roman way Via Claudia Augusta.

AV2 traverses shady woodland on its way to Paradis

clearing dotted with old huts, some still with original stone-slab roof tiles.

Here it's sharp R on a narrow quiet road that wastes no time heading downhill, with views to the valley floor and AV2's destination. Along the way you touch on hamlets made up of clusters of old houses with traditional timber balconies, flourishing gardens, drinking fountains and meadows.

Norcen (489m) boasts a prominent church and sizeable settlement, including a modest *trattoria* if you're tempted by lunch. A couple of bends downhill is the yellow Casa Alpina San Marco building, where AV2 branches L on a grassy path – a brief respite from tarmac. You soon return to the road and proceed to nearby **Pedavena** (335m, **1hr 30min**). ◄

> The village square has shops, eateries and buses to Feltre.

Straight ahead, a short way along the tree-lined Viale Vittorio Veneto, is the historic Birreria where they've been brewing beer since 1897 (https://labirreriapedavena.it). The bustling restaurant and rambling gardens beckon you in.

To complete the final 3km, proceed SE on the avenue, which changes name a couple of times. It passes through the lower part of the beautiful walled Renaissance town of **Feltre** (274m) – definitely worth an exploratory wander. (Detour L through the arch signed for the *centro storico* and its frescoed palaces). ◄

> In August a marvellous medieval Palio celebration is held here, with horse races and street dining; the whole town dons costumes.

Remember to present your *rifugi* stamps at the tourist office for your well-earned AV2 badge (Piazza Vittorio Emanuele II, 21, tel 0439 2540).

Accommodation includes the centrally located **B&B Bus de l'Och** (tel 0439 81322, **www.busdeloch.it**) and Hotel Garnì la Cuba (tel 0439 310568, **www.hotelgarnilacuba.it**; between Pedavena and Feltre).

The road swings R out to the railway station (**45min**). Trentino Trasporti buses run to Trento for rail connections back to Bressanone if needed; otherwise take a train S via Treviso to Venice.

ALTE VIE 3–6

The jagged Tre Cime can be admired on AV4

Alta Via 3

Start	Villabassa
Finish	Longarone
Distance	100km
Grade	Grade 2–3 with numerous short aided sections
Time	45hr – 8 days
Highest point	2378m
Maps	Kompass 1:35,000 sheets 3+4, n.672 four-map pack; Tabacco 1:25,000 sheets 031, 03, 025
Access	Villabassa, in Val Pusteria, can be reached by train and SAD bus; Longarone at the end has trains on the Venice–Calalzo line and Dolomiti Bus runs to Belluno.
Note	Sleeping and via ferrata equipment and experience are needed for the concluding sections after Rifugio Bosconero.

The Alta Via dei Camosci (chamois) begins with particularly long but rewarding days rambling past the magnificent Cristallo and Sorapiss massifs. After veering over the Boite valley near Cortina d'Ampezzo it touches on the mighty Pelmo and modest Monte Rite – a superb lookout. Then it traverses the rugged solitary Sfornioi-Bosconero group with a sequence of challenging exposed passages, mostly aided, before the trek conclusion at Longarone in the Piave valley – a key traffic artery. Overnight stays are in refuges and guesthouses, then in a spartan bivouac hut on the last night.

Beginning at **Villabassa** (1153m) near the railway station, AV3 strikes out on road at first across farmland and woods, preparing itself for a tiring series of ups and downs on very narrow paths over little-frequented ridges. Passing a smidgen below the summit of **Picco di Vallandro**, it reaches **Pratopiazza** (1991m, **7hr**), where wonderful meadows give views to Croda Rossa. Rifugio Pratopiazza (tel 0474 748650, www.plaetzwiese.com); Hotel Hohe Gaisl (tel 0474 748606, www.hohegaisl. com). Further on, and brilliantly placed for admiring

Villabassa
↓
7h
↓
Pratopiazza
↓
30min
↓
Rif Vallandro
↓
2h 30min
↓
Landro
↓
5h 30min
↓
Passo Tre Croci
↓
2h
↓
Rif Vandelli
↓
2h 30min
↓
Rif Capanna Tondi
↓
2h
↓
Zuel
↓
2h
↓
San Vito di Cadore
↓
3h 30min
↓
Rif Venezia
↓
4h 30min
↓
Monte Rite
↓
1h 30min
↓
Passo Cibiana
↓
3h 30min
↓
Rif Bosconero
↓
5h
↓
Biv Tovanella
↓
3h
↓
Longarone

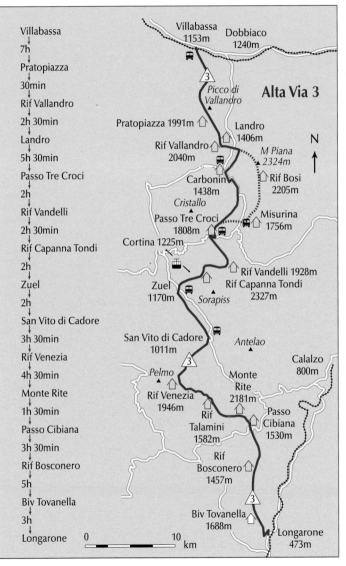

Villabassa 1153m

Dobbiaco 1240m

Alta Via 3

Picco di Vallandro

Pratopiazza 1991m

Landro 1406m

Rif Vallandro 2040m

M Piana 2324m

N

Carbonin 1438m

Rif Bosi 2205m

Cristallo

Passo Tre Croci 1808m

Misurina 1756m

Cortina 1225m

Rif Vandelli 1928m

Zuel 1170m

Rif Capanna Tondi 2327m

Sorapiss

San Vito di Cadore 1011m

Antelao

Calalzo 800m

Pelmo

Monte Rite 2181m

Rif Venezia 1946m

Rif Talamini 1582m

Passo Cibiana 1530m

Rif Bosconero 1457m

Biv Tovanella 1688m

Longarone 473m

0   10
km

sunsets on the Cristallo, is **Rifugio Vallandro** (2040m, **30min**; tel 0474 972505, www.vallandro.it).

After climbing to a saddle close to Monte Specie, AV3 plunges helter-skelter to the valley floor at **Landro** (1406m, **2hr 30min**), with accommodation at Hotel Drei Zinnen (tel 0474 972633, www.hoteltrecime.com). ◄

A SAD bus can be taken from here to Misurina, where a change to Dolomiti Bus links to Passo Tre Croci.

Variant via Misurina

An interesting option, which avoids the section of road-walking after Carbonin, branches off at Landro. It follows the narrow, airy Sentiero dei Pionieri ascending **Monte Piano** (2324m) – an open-air WW1 museum. It's not far on to **Rifugio Bosi** (2205m, tel 0435 39034, https://rifugiobosimontepiana.business.site). A wide track then drops to **Misurina** (1752m, hotels, ATM, groceries) and its pretty lake where you take the link path for ex **Rifugio Popena**, thence **Passo Tre Croci** as described below).

Now a broad cycle track, the former railway line leads past Lago di Landro to **Carbonin** (1438m), which consists of a café, hotel Croda Rossa (tel 379 1942085, www.hotelcrodarossa.eu) and apartments Villaggio Ploner (http://villaggioploner.it). Then, a short distance up the Misurina road, take the branch along Val Popena Alta that becomes a tiring climb to the spectacularly located – but unfortunately derelict – Rifugio Popena (2214m).

From an adjoining saddle, an initially eroded tract reinforced with walkways and steps makes its gradual way to the road and on to **Passo Tre Croci** (1808m, **5hr 30min**). Café-restaurant and rooms at B&B Hotel Tre Croci (tel 0436 1996180, cortina@hotelbb.com).

A leisurely track cuts across the fossil-studded flanks of Cime Marcoira to a beautiful amphitheatre with a pretty turquoise lake in the shadow of the Sorapiss, and **Rifugio Vandelli** (1928m, **2hr**; tel 0435 39015, www.rifugiovandelli.it, CAI, late June to late Sept).

Now a series of aided passages climbs to Forcella Ciadin (2378m), the highest point reached on the trek. A lovely traverse with vast views over the Cortina Dolomites brings you to **Rifugio Capanna Tondi** (2327m, **2hr 30min**;

tel 0436 5775, info@rifugiocapannatondi.it, mid June to mid Sept).

Not far downhill is the cable-car to Cortina and Rifugio Faloria (tel 0436 2737, https://faloriacristallo.it), but AV3 drops down Val Orita on a steep path into woodland. This concludes at **Zuel** (1170m, **2hr**) and the main road. ▶ Purists who aren't taking the bus will cross the road and head for the village of Socol, where a track continues on the other side of Torrente Boite, ending up in the spread-out resort of **San Vito di Cadore** (1010m, **2hr**) with hotels and shops.

On surfaced road as far as the houses of Serdes, AV3 then follows a jeep track that ascends relentlessly through woods, finally emerging to flowered meadows and **Rifugio Venezia** (1946m, **3hr 30min**; tel 0436 9684, www.rifugiovenezia.it, CAI, late June to late Sept). ▶

With a decisive swing around Monte Pena by way of minor saddles, a lane is joined to **Rifugio Talamini** (1582m; tel 380 9081496, www.rifugiogptalamini.com,

Rifugio Vandelli and its gorgeous lake are mere dots below the Sorapiss

Here a Dolomiti Bus can be caught to San Vito di Cadore.

Rifugio Venezia stands at the foot of the 'throne of the gods': the breathtaking Pelmo.

Rifugio Venezia is dwarfed by the mighty Pelmo

open year-round) before gaining height on a traverse to **Monte Rite** (2181m, **4hr 30min**). Here a World War 1 fort has been converted into a museum and Rifugio Dolomites (tel 348 5658675, www.rifugiomonterite.it, June to Sept).

A winding 7km former military road terminates at **Passo Cibiana** (1530m, **1hr 30min**) and Rifugio Remauro (tel 348 6906457, www.rifugioremauro.it) as well as restaurant/guesthouse Baita Deona (tel 0435 540169, www. baitadeona.it). ◄

A shuttle bus runs down the military road Jun–Sept.

Through a clutch of old *tabià* (haymaking) huts it's a steady ascent to Forcella de le Ciavazole (1994m) in the rugged Sfornioi group, thence a knee-testing descent across vast scree spreads to **Rifugio Bosconero** (1457m, **3hr 30min**; tel 338 3713870, https://rifugiobosconero.it, CAI, June to mid Sept).

At this point walkers not in possession of the equipment, food and experience required for the concluding two days should bail out here – path n.490-491 traverses and drops to Forno (803m) in Val Zoldana (2hr) where there are Dolomiti Bus runs to Longarone.

It's steep going beneath Sasso di Bosconero towards Forcella de la Tovanella (2150m), along jagged ridges over wild Val Tovanella, with a series of tricky passages and narrow ledges – routes forged by intrepid chamois hunters.

After Forcella di Viàz de le Ponte (1909m) and guiding chains down a chimney, the immense scree basin Vant de la Serra is crossed with a difficult exposed ledge and a hands-on scramble. ▶ Easier terrain leads down to the spartan premises of converted herders' hut **Bivacco Tovanella** (1688m, **5hr**), with beds for eight and a tank of rainwater.

Immediately after Porta de la Serra (2050m) is a plaque in memory of Brovelli and Tolot, inventors of the AV3.

Following an initial climb to 1840m, straightforward paths continue high over Val del Maé, with vast outlooks and a string of old huts. Steady descent leads to a surfaced road near the village of Podenzoi (799m). A final hour downhill means the conclusion of AV3 at **Longarone** (473m, **3hr**) and a well-deserved cool drink at a café-restaurant or a hotel stay.

Longarone is renowned for its creamy *gelato* (ice cream) – but also for the 1963 Vajont Dam tragedy in which 1917 people were drowned by a tidal wave generated when Monte Toc collapsed into the lake across the valley.

Alta Via 4

Start	San Candido
Finish	Pieve di Cadore
Distance	85km
Grade	Grade 2–3 with long, exposed aided sections and vie ferrate
Time	33hr 30min – 6 days
Highest point	2624m
Maps	Kompass 1:35,000 sheet 3, n.672 four-map pack; Tabacco 1:25,000 sheets 010, 03, 016
Access	San Candido, in Val Pusteria, has trains and SAD buses; at the end, Pieve di Cadore has Dolomiti Bus runs to Calalzo (trains), and Cortina Express to Venice.
Note	Via ferrata gear and experience essential for the Cadini and Marmarole sections.

Established in 1973 by Toni Sanmarchi (who also did AV5), AV4 was subtitled the 'Alta Via di Paul Grohmann' for the Viennese mountaineer who first scaled the Tre Scarperi, Cima Grande di Lavaredo, Sorapiss and Antelao – all of which punctuate the route. AV4 begins its trans-Dolomite journey in the spectacular Sesto group with good paths, a host of breathtaking vistas and a string of popular refuges. Then airy aided ways take over, threading through the Cadini line-up of spires. Opposite are the rugged Marmarole, explored on lengthy, thrilling aided scrambles where experience is a must. The trek wraps up with a wander around the soaring pyramid Antelao, before descending to the elegant alpine township of Pieve di Cadore, birthplace of great Renaissance artist Titian. Overnight stays are in well-run refuges and one tiny bivouac hut.

From historic **San Candido** (1174m) the 4km to café-restaurant **Alte Säge** (**45min**) can be covered either on foot via a lane or by the SAD bus. Here, AV4 penetrates the Sesto Dolomites by way of Val Campo di Dentro. ◄

A midsummer shuttle runs partway up.

Woods and meadows accompany to **Rifugio Tre Scarperi** (1626m, **2hr**; tel 0474 966610, www.

San Candido
↓
2h 45min
↓
Rif Tre Scarperi
↓
3h
↓
Rif Locatelli
↓
2h
↓
Rif Auronzo
↓
3h
↓
Rif Fonda Savio
↓
1h 30min
↓
Rif Col de Varda
↓
1h
↓
Misurina
↓
1h 45min
↓
Passo Tre Croci
↓
2h
↓
Rif Vandelli
↓
4h
↓
Biv Comici
↓
4h
↓
Rif San Marco
↓
1h 30min
↓
Rif Galassi
↓
5h
↓
Rif Antelao
↓
2h
↓
Pieve di Cadore

Alta Via 4

N
↑

Dobbiaco 1240m
San Candido 1174m

Rif Tre Scarperi 1626m
Tre Scarperi

Rif Locatelli 2405m
Tre Cime
Rif Auronzo 2320m

Rif Fonda Savio 2367m

Carbonin 1438m
Cristallo
Misurina 1752m
Cadini

Passo Tre Croci 1808m
Rif Col de Varda 2115m

Cortina
Rif Vandelli 1926m
Biv Comici 2050m
Marmarole
Sorapiss

Rif San Marco 1823m
Rif Galassi 2018m
San Vito di Cadore
Antelao
Rif Antelao 1796m
Calalzo

Pieve di Cadore 880m

0   10 km

drei-schuster-huette.com, AVS, June to Sept), where Tyrolean gastronomic specialities are the order of the day.

Clear paths climb beneath a stunning line-up of peaks to a vast plateau to admire the magnificent Tre Cime di Lavaredo from **Rifugio Locatelli** (2405m, **3hr**; tel 0474 972002, www.dreizinnenhuette.com, CAI, late June to Sept). Then an old wartime mule track drops via Pian del Rin as it circles the magnificent three via Col di Mezzo (2324m) to a road and **Rifugio Auronzo** (2320m, **2hr**; tel 0435 39002, www.rifugioauronzo.it, CAI, June to Sept). ◀

SAD and Dolomiti Bus services to Misurina and beyond.

Maintaining altitude, AV4 now follows Sentiero Bonacossa, a WW1 route along the central ridge of the Cadini, dodging elegant rock needles. Cables, a tunnel, ladders, rungs and panoramic ledges lead to Forcella de Rinbianco (2176m), under Torre Wundt. From there an easier path follows a marvellous valley climbing steeply to **Rifugio Fonda Savio** (2367m, **3hr**; tel 0435 39036, www.fonda-savio.it, CAI, June to Sept).

In a similar vein the path continues in the direction of an imposing rock tower to Forcella del Diavolo (2598m) and across the Ciadin de la Neve snowfield. More aided

Crossing the Sesto Dolomites

passages cross rubble gullies, then a straightforward path concludes at **Rifugio Col de Varda** (2115m, **1hr 30min**; tel 0435 39041, http://rifugiocoldevarda.it, June to Sept).

Either follow the lane or ride the chair lift down to **Misurina** (1752m, **1hr**; hotels, groceries), where a beautiful lake reflects majestic peaks. Then allow **1hr 45min** on foot along the road for the 6km journey to **Passo Tre Croci** (1808m). ▸

A ride on the Dolomiti Bus is the best way to cover this stretch of tarmac.

In common with AV3, a leisurely track cuts beneath Cime Marcoira to a stunning amphitheatre with a pretty turquoise lake, and **Rifugio Vandelli** (1926m, **2hr**; tel 0435 39015, www.rifugiovandelli.it, CAI, late June to late Sept). ▸

The breathtaking Sorapiss towers overhead.

Now for the full-blooded via ferrata Vandelli, curving high over Val d'Ansiei. Fitted with ladders, rungs and cable, it makes for an exciting climb to 2370m over Col del Fuoco via chimneys, ledges and sheer rock faces. Shrubby vegetation and grass reappear in the basin Busa del Banco, where you drop via steep flanks to **Bivacco Comici** (2050m, **4hr**) which sleeps nine.

Dizzily high over Val di San Vito, the Sentiero Minazio entails more aided exposed passages and difficulty en route to magnificent Forcella Grande (2255m) at the foot of Torre Sabbioni, in the Marmarole range now. It's a short but tiring descent to the welcoming **Rifugio San Marco** (1823m, **4hr**; tel 0436 9444, www.rifugio sanmarco.com, CAI, late June to late Sept). ▸

Exit path to San Vito di Cadore, 1hr 30min.

Over eroding terrain, a clear path now cuts across to Forcella Piccola (2120m) and the converted barracks **Rifugio Galassi** (2018m, **1hr 30min**; tel 340 1214300, www.rifugiogalassi.it, CAI, June to Sept).

In the shadow of the giant pyramidal Antelao, AV4 proceeds over tiring moraine then up a rock face to Forcella del Ghiacciaio (2584m) and the sight of ice domes on the shrinking glacier. A steep, tricky chimney drops to grass and light woods in Val Antelao.

Once Forcella Piria (2096m) is gained, with vast views to the Duranno-Cima dei Preti groups, it's easy going past the Crode di San Pietro and on to the comfortable **Rifugio**

Rifugio Galassi at the foot of Antelao

Antelao (1796m, **5hr**; tel 0435 75333 or 392 1196841, liviozanardo2410@gmail.com, CAI, June to Oct).

A jeep track leads via Forcella Antracisa (1693m), where it's best to avoid Monte Tranego and choose the path to Pozzale (1054m) and its modest piazza with a café. Then it's 1.6km down the road to **Pieve di Cadore** (880m, **2hr**) for hotels, restaurants and Dolomiti Bus transport.

Alta Via 5

Start	Sesto
Finish	Pieve di Cadore
Distance	90km
Grade	Grade 2–3 with extended exposed, aided sections and vie ferrate
Time	38hr – 7 days
Highest point	2650m
Maps	Kompass 1:35,000 sheet 3, n.672 four-map pack; Tabacco 1:25,000 sheets 010, 017, 016
Access	Sesto, in an eastern branch of Val Pusteria, is served by SAD buses; at the other end Pieve di Cadore has Dolomiti Bus runs to Calalzo (trains), and Cortina Express to Venice.
Note	Via ferrata gear and experience essential for the Marmarole section.

Running parallel to AV4, this trek similarly concludes at Pieve di Cadore – birthplace of Renaissance artist Titian, who immortalised these landscapes in his canvases, thus the dedication Alta Via di Tiziano. After traversing the magnificent and popular Sesto Dolomites with comfortable refuges, AV5 drops across the Auronzo valley to embark on an arduous, solitary and highly rewarding exploration of the wild Marmarole range. This means a sequence of tough interlinked aided routes and bivouac huts, with the occasional manned refuge. Take food, cooking and sleeping gear and be aware that water is scarce.

From **Sesto** (1302m) on foot it's 3km to the opening of beautiful Val Fiscalina and Dolomitenhof (1454m, **30min**), but SAD buses also run this far. Through flowered meadows flanking the mammoth Tre Scarperi, a lane quickly reaches Rifugio Fondo Valle (1548m; tel 0474 710606, www.talschlusshuette.com, May to Oct).

With a vast choice of dramatic mountains to admire, AV5 now climbs steadily to **Rifugio Zsigmondy-Comici** (2224m, **2hr**; tel 0474 710358, www.zsigmondyhuette.

com, June to Oct), magnificently located opposite Monte Popera.

The scree-filled head of Val Fiscalina Alta is traversed to Forcella Giralba (2431m), thence quiet **Rifugio Carducci** (2297m, **1hr**; tel 347 6861580, www.rifugio carducci.eu, CAI, June to Oct). A long, tiring descent ensues alongside an ice-blue torrent and through woods dwarfed by soaring rock walls, with the path emerging on the road at **Giralba** (935m, **2hr 30min**).

Only 1.5km downstream is Ligonto with Albergo Ristorante Cacciatori (tel 0435 97017 www.albergo-ristorante-cacciatori.com). Soon the Torrente Ansiei is crossed and a minor road leads up pastoral Valle da Rin to café-eatery La Primula (1060m, **1hr 15min**). From here, heading decidedly uphill to cut across the easternmost corner of the Marmarole, AV5 climbs an eroded gully to panoramic Forcella Paradiso (2045m), thence cosy **Rifugio Ciareido** (1969m, **4hr**; tel 0435 76276, www.rifugiociareido.com, May to Oct).

A straightforward path through a sea of dwarf mountain pines goes to **Rifugio Baion** (1828m, **45min**; tel 0435 76060, www.rifugiobaion.it, CAI, June to Sept). AV5 now skirts rugged mountains including Croda Bianca, aided by short stretches of cable over outcrops. Forcella Sacu (1914m, **2hr**) is reached in a clearing. (Only a 20min detour away is **Rifugio Chiggiato** (1911m; tel 346 1817182, www.rifugiochiggiato.it, CAI, late June to late Sept).

Cables help walkers up the rock face en route to Forcella Sacu

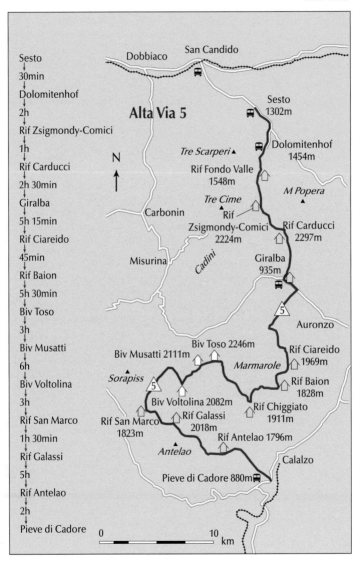

Sesto
↓ 30min
Dolomitenhof
↓ 2h
Rif Zsigmondy-Comici
↓ 1h
Rif Carducci
↓ 2h 30min
Giralba
↓ 5h 15min
Rif Ciareido
↓ 45min
Rif Baion
↓ 5h 30min
Biv Toso
↓ 3h
Biv Musatti
↓ 6h
Biv Voltolina
↓ 3h
Rif San Marco
↓ 1h 30min
Rif Galassi
↓ 5h
Rif Antelao
↓ 2h
Pieve di Cadore

Alta Via 5

Dobbiaco   San Candido

Sesto 1302m

Dolomitenhof 1454m

Tre Scarperi ▲

Rif Fondo Valle 1548m

M Popera ▲

Tre Cime ▲ Rif

Carbonin

Zsigmondy-Comici 2224m

Rif Carducci 2297m

Misurina   *Cadini*

Giralba 935m

Rif Ciareido 1969m

Auronzo

Biv Toso 2246m

Biv Musatti 2111m   *Marmarole*

Sorapiss ▲

Rif Baion 1828m

Biv Voltolina 2082m

Rif Chiggiato 1911m

Rif San Marco 1823m   Rif Galassi 2018m

Rif Antelao 1796m

Antelao ▲   Calalzo

Pieve di Cadore 880m

0   10 km

125

Soon AV5 becomes vertical and joins a via ferrata with lengths of cable to reach Forcella Jau de la Tana (2650m) and brilliant views. This leads down into the hidden world of the Lastoni delle Marmarole – vast eroded rock slabs where orientation can be tricky in low visibility. A well looked-after metal cabin with beds for nine, **Bivacco Toso** (2246m, **3hr 30min**), stands alongside the historic stone Rifugio Tiziano (locked; for CAI members only). Water can be found 30min downhill.

A faint route ascends Val Longa, making its way up the Tacco del Todesco ridge. Hands-on and aided ledge passages lead to a 2614m saddle with a brilliant outlook. A bit more clambering on the 'Strada Sanmarchi' concludes in the desolate basin Meduce di Fuori, where snow lies late. Here stands **Bivacco Musatti** (2111m, **3hr**), another essential metallic shelter which sleeps nine.

Especially difficult and tiring climbing passages come next, on the approach to Forcella del Mescol (2400m), and across the head of Meduce di Dentro, a solitary cirque. Ladders and a precious water source are encountered on the approach to unworldly Forcella di Croda Rotta (2569m).

A challenging narrow crest and ledges lead to dizzy Forcella Vanedel (2372m), and then further cable-aided sections round the Croda de Marchi to more ledges. From a stream (alias water supply) it's not far to red cabin **Bivacco Voltolina** (2082m, **6hr**, beds for nine) in the vast amphitheatre of Van di Scotter.

The Corno del Doge is rounded on an exposed natural ledge, with the help of cable. After several tricky points, you join a path in Val di San Vito then climb in the shade of Torre Sabbioni to reach Forcella Grande (2255m). It's a short steep way down to the welcoming **Rifugio San Marco** (1823m, **3hr**; tel 0436 9444, www.rifugiosanmarco.com, CAI, late June to late Sept).

From here on the trek is in common with AV4 – see above. This entails **1hr 30min** to **Rifugio Galassi** (2018m), a further **5hr** to **Rifugio Antelao** (1796m) and a concluding **2hr** to **Pieve di Cadore** (880m).

Alta Via 6

Start	Rifugio Sorgenti del Piave (Sappada)
Finish	Vittorio Veneto
Distance	190km
Grade	Grade 2–3 with long exposed sections, some aided, and difficult terrain where orientation can be a problem
Time	62hr 30min – 11 days
Highest point	2217m
Maps	Tabacco 1:25,000 sheets 01, 02, 021, 012, 024
Access	The closest bus stop is Cima Sappada (1236m), reachable by Dolomiti Bus from Calalzo (trains) and Arriva runs from Tolmezzo. Allow an extra 3hr for the 6km up Val Sesis on paths and tarmac to reach the trek start. Vittorio Veneto at the trek finish is on the Venice–Calalzo train line.
Note	Via ferrata gear and experience are essential for the central sections.

Fascinating if challenging and protracted, 'Alta Via dei Silenzi' explores the spectacular little-trodden eastern fringe of the Dolomites, safeguarded under the Parco Naturale delle Dolomiti Friulane. Beginning at the source of the Piave river, it runs parallel to the key eponymous valley. On the gently paced opening days it crosses the Cridola, Spalti di Toro–Monfalconi groups with a decent scattering of refuges. Next, AV6 tramps through the rugged Duranno–Cima dei Preti where paths become fainter and accommodation spartan. The going can be rugged. After the village of Erto comes less dramatic, medium-altitude Col Nudo–Cavallo and fair distances along asphalted road. Next comes the Alpago district, followed by the Cansiglio plateau, renowned for its dairy products and carefully nurtured forests. Centuries ago, immense rafts of timber harvested here were piloted downstream to the lagoon city of Venice, for use in foundations and in shipbuilding.

It goes without saying that walkers need to be fit, experienced, self-sufficient and well equipped.

From **Rifugio Sorgenti del Piave** (1815m; tel 334 779 9175, June to Sept) a panoramic path climbs easily over gullies leading to Passo del Mulo (2356m) surrounded

Inspiring scenery near Passo del Mulo

by trenches and reminders of WW1. Well below the clutch of Laghi d'Olbe (tarns, 2156m) is Ristorante Gosse (1847m, **3hr**) from where linked chair lifts glide downhill – an alternative to the monotonous jeep track that concludes at charming spread-out **Sappada** (1240m, **1hr 30min** on foot). Groceries, accommodation including Pensione Fontana (tel 0435 469174, www.hotel fontanasappada.it).

From Granvilla in the western part of the village, AV6 ventures along the wooded Enghe valley, branching off via waterfalls to Passo Elbel (1963m). A traverse high over Val Pesarina entails eroded passages via the Clap Piccolo clearing (1623m) before the route approaches **Clap Grande** and **Rifugio Fratelli De Gasperi** (1767m, **4hr 30min**; tel 366 1745882, www.rifdegasperi.it, CAI, June to Sept).

You backtrack to Clap Piccolo for a long, gradual descent via Forcella Lavardet (1491m). Quiet surfaced roads and lanes lead up and down through woods and meadows, finally gaining friendly **Rifugio Fabbro** (1783m, **4hr**; tel 0435 460357, rifugiofabbro@libero.it) which faces Monte Tudaio.

After a 3km stretch of tarmac, AV6 heads along a lane to the scenically placed summer farm Casera Doana (1911m). Cutting over Col Rosolo on forest pathways, it veers sharply over Alta Val del Tagliamento, joining a lane to **Passo della Mauria** (1298m, **4hr**), where there is a café-restaurant. ▶

A lane breaks off, soon becoming a path through woods, open mountainsides and over streams on a roller-coaster route to **Rifugio Giaf** (1400m, **2hr**; tel 338 7856338, https://rifugiogiaf.org, CAI, June to Sept).

Steady ascent into inspirational rockscapes and a cirque conclude at Forcella Scodavacca (2043m) under Monte Cridola. Take a breather before the plunge to the Pra' de Toro meadows and cosy **Rifugio Padova** (1278m, **3hr**; tel 0435 72488 or 338 4763400, www.rifugio padova.it, CAI, May to Oct), at the foot of the elegant rocky crests of the Spalti di Toro–Monfalconi.

AV6 continues over a knoll to cross bridged streams before a steady climb to Casera Vedorcia (1704m) – a dairy farm-cum-belvedere. Not far up is the delightful

The road pass has SAF buses going in both directions – to Calalzo or Tolmezzo.

Charming old house at Sappada

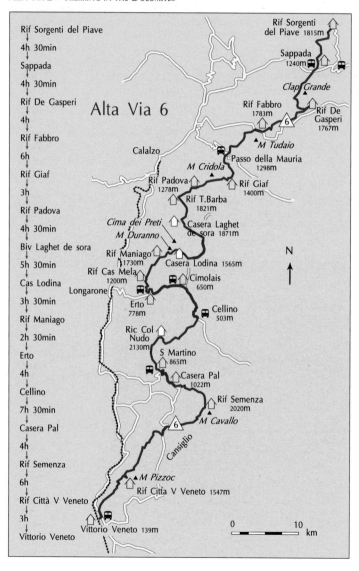

Rif Sorgenti del Piave

↓ 4h 30min

Sappada

↓ 4h 30min

Rif De Gasperi

↓ 4h

Rif Fabbro

↓ 6h

Rif Giaf

↓ 3h

Rif Padova

↓ 4h 30min

Biv Laghet de sora

↓ 5h 30min

Cas Lodina

↓ 3h 30min

Rif Maniago

↓ 2h 30min

Erto

↓ 4h

Cellino

↓ 7h 30min

Casera Pal

↓ 4h

Rif Semenza

↓ 6h

Rif Città V Veneto

↓ 3h

Vittorio Veneto

Alta Via 6

Rif Sorgenti del Piave 1815m

Sappada 1240m

Clap Grande

Rif Fabbro 1783m

Rif De Gasperi 1767m

M Tudaio

Passo della Mauria 1298m

Calalzo

M Cridola

Rif Padova 1278m

Rif Giaf 1400m

Rif T.Barba 1821m

Cima dei Preti

M Duranno

Casera Laghet de sora 1871m

Rif Maniago 1730m

Casera Lodina 1565m

Rif Cas Mela 1200m

Cimolais 650m

Longarone

Erto 778m

Cellino 503m

Ric Col Nudo 2130m

S Martino 865m

Casera Pal 1022m

Rif Semenza 2020m

M Cavallo

Cansiglio

M Pizzoc

Rif Citta V Veneto 1547m

Vittorio Veneto 139m

N ↑

0   10 km

log cabin **Rifugio Tita Barba** (1821m, **2hr**, tel 0435 32902 or 392 7281781, rifugiotitabarba@gmail.com, June to Sept).

Nearly at Forcella Scodavacca

By all means exit here to Calalzo and the railway station if you're not equipped for the tougher stuff that follows.

It's straightforward going to Forcella Spè (2049m), the gateway to Val Cimoliana. Rugged Val Misera and Valle dei Lares are crossed in quick succession, before an outcrop is rounded to reach Val del Frassin, where the lovely cabin **Bivacco Casera Laghet de sora** (1871m, **2hr 30min**, sleeps eight) stands in a veritable botanical garden, with water nearby.

From here, the original AV6 proceeded via Forcella Val dei Drap (2290m, 2hr), Forcella dei Cacciatori (2173m), Forcella Compol (2450m, 4hr) then Bivacco Greselin (1920m, 2hr) to Forcella Duranno (2217m, 2hr), with the drawn-out exposed and difficult sequences being restricted to experienced climbers. However, storm damage and deterioration has since led to path closures for safety reasons, so the trek has been rerouted as follows.

AV6 now embarks on a mammoth 1300+m descent down Val del Frassin to the floor of Val Cimoliana (929m, **2hr**). After a 5.5km jaunt down the minor road to the Ponte Campol bridge (728m, **1hr**) comes a hefty uphill through woodland to the cosy stone hut **Casera Lodina** (1565m, **2hr 30min**, sleeps six, water on the approach path). Here the trees are left behind and marvellous views to Monte Duranno and Cima dei Preti can be enjoyed.

Continue up to Forcella Lodina (1853m), followed by a mostly straightforward path with a little exposure to Forcella Duranno (2217m). A steep, scrambly descent over rock into the trees concludes at homely **Rifugio Maniago** (1730m, **3hr 30min**, tel 0427 667027 or 338 1697479, 1965picozzi@gmail.com, CAI, June to Oct).

Sadly, Erto was involved in the 1963 Vajont disaster when neighbouring Monte Toc slid into a dammed lake, generating a gigantic destructive wave.

It's easy walking down to the rough road in Val Zemola via a summer farm with food and beds, **Rifugio Casera Mela** (1200m, tel 338 7857908, www.casera mela.it, June to Sept). Further on is the village of **Erto** (778m, **2hr 30min**). ◀ Shops, B&Bs (Emma tel 0427 879006 or Dromì tel 0427 879261, www.ertoecasso.it).

Exit route
To exit here, the ATAP bus can be taken W to Longarone (12km) for onward trains.

AV6 now heads E for 13.5km (**4hr**) by road. By all means save time by catching the bus via **Cimolais** (650m, shops, Albergo Ristorante Alla Rosa restaurant/hostel, tel 0427 87061) to **Cellino** (503m). Now heading towards Col Nudo, take the lane up Valle Chialedina through woodland, gaining height all of a sudden. En route is the tiny emergency shelter Casera Gravuzza (984m), tucked into the mountainside. Then rock steps and cable help gain the crest and Passo di Valbona (2130m, **5hr**) with **Ricovero di Col Nudo**, a cave overhang fitted out as a bivouac for four; there's water inside.

Heading past curious naturally sculpted outcrops, AV6 continues downhill to the minor pass of Scalet Bassa (1169m) and a surfaced road, in the Alpago district now. By way of **San Martino** (865m, meals and accommodation at Locanda San Martino, tel 334 1390806, www.locanda-san-martino.it; bus to Belluno) and Funes (817m), it reaches Tamera (914m). A shortcut joins a final stretch of road to a summer farm and eatery with accommodation: **Agriturismo Casera Pal** (1022m, **2hr 30min**, tel 329 4428227, www.caserapal.it).

AV6 now follows a track heading along karstic Val Salatis, then Valle Sperlonga to reach Forcella Laste on Monte Cavallo and the scenically placed **Rifugio Semenza** (2020m, **4hr**; tel 0437 49055, benetti.nadia@ alice.it, CAI, June to Sept).

A panoramic path through a cirque ends at a der-elict farm, Casera Palatina (1521m), then good paths lead to the hamlet of Canaie and Val Tritton, followed by a short stretch of tarmac to Campon (1040m, **1hr 30min**). ▸ Here a road closed to traffic curves around to Palughetto and meets a lane which ascends through woodland to Col Mazzuc and across to the panoramic crest high over the **Cansiglio** forest and pastoral basin.

Buses available.

Having crossed Pian de la Pita and passed Monte Millifret, the Casere Pizzoc turn-off (1499m) is finally reached – it's a short worthwhile detour to **Monte Pizzoc** and the rambling **Rifugio Città di Vittorio Veneto** (1547m, **4hr 30min**; tel 0438 1642595, www.rifugio cittadivittorioveneto.it, May to Sept).

Back at the turn-off, AV6 begins the long gradual descent by way of Agnelezza and its farm, then a lane to a small quarry. A path along wooded Costa di Serravalle drops to the chapel of Sant'Augusta (350m) for a paved lane into Serravalle, the charming Renaissance part of **Vittorio Veneto** (139m, **3hr**). Cafés, hotels, restaurants, as well as trains and buses, are only a short stroll away.

APPENDIX A
Useful contacts

Tourist information
The Italian Tourist Board (www.italia.it) has offices all over the world and inspiring websites crammed with helpful info for intending travellers.

UK (London office)
tel 020 74081254

Australia (Sydney office)
tel 02 93572561
https://visitaly.com.au

USA (New York office)
tel (212) 2455618
www.italiantourism.com

In the Dolomites, local tourist offices useful for Alte Vie 2–6 are as follows. To phone Italy from abroad, use the country code +39 and include the initial '0' when dialling a landline.

Auronzo
tel 0435 400078
https://auronzomisurina.it

Belluno
tel 334 2813222
http://adorable.belluno.it

Bressanone
tel 0472 275252
www.brixen.org

Cortina d'Ampezzo
tel 0436 869086
www.dolomiti.org

Dobbiaco
tel 0474 972132
www.dobbiaco.bz

Falcade
tel 0437 599062
www.dolomiti.org

Feltre
tel 0439 2540
www.visitfeltre.info

Fiera di Primiero
tel 0439 62407
www.sanmartino.com

Longarone
tel 0437 770119
www.prolocolongarone.it

Misurina
tel 0435 39016
https://auronzomisurina.it

Moena
tel 0462 609770
www.fassa.com

Pieve di Cadore
tel 0435 500257
www.dolomiti.org

San Andrea
tel 0472 850008
www.brixen.org

San Candido
tel 0474 913149
www.tre-cime.info

San Martino di Castrozza
tel 0439 768867
www.sanmartino.com

Santa Cristina
tel 0471 777800
www.valgardena.it

San Vito di Cadore
tel 0436 9238
www.dolomiti.org

Sappada
tel 0435 469131
www.turismofvg.it

Sesto
tel 0474 710310
www.tre-cime.info

Villabassa
tel 0474 745136
www.tre-cime.info

Vittorio Veneto
tel 0438 57243
www.turismovittorioveneto.it

Parks on Alte Vie 2–6
Parco Naturale Dolomiti Friulane
www.parcodolomitifriulane.it

Parco Naturale Fanes-Senes-Braies,
Puez-Odle, Dolomiti di Sesto
https://nature-parks.provinz.bz.it

Parco Naturale Paneveggio Pale di San
Martino
https://www.parcopan.org

Parco Nazionale delle Dolomiti
Bellunesi
www.dolomitipark.it

Transport

Trains
Austrian Rail
www.oebb.at

Eurostar
www.eurostar.com

France
www.sncf.com

Germany
www.bahn.com

Italy
www.trenitalia.com

Buses
Arriva
https://tplfvg.it/it

ATAP
www.atap.pn.it

ATVO
www.atvo.it

Cortina Express
www.cortinaexpress.it

Dolomiti Bus
www.dolomitibus.it

SAD
www.sad.it

Trentino Trasporti
www.trentinotrasporti.it

Airports
Treviso
www.trevisoairport.it

Venice
www.veniceairport.com

Verona
www.aeroportoverona.it

Weather
Südtirol
https://weather.provinz.bz.it

Trentino
www.meteotrentino.it

Veneto
www.arpa.veneto.it

Emergencies
General emergency
tel 112

Soccorso alpino (mountain rescue)
tel 118

APPENDIX B
Italian–English glossary

Italian	English
acqua (non) potabile	water (not) suitable for drinking
agriturismo	farm with meals and/or accommodation
aiuto!	help!
albergo	hotel
alimentari	grocery shop
alpe	mountain pasture
alto	high
altopiano/ altipiano	high altitude plateau, upland
aperto	open
autostazione	bus station
bagno	bathroom or toilet
baita	alpine shepherd's hut, sometimes a farm or refuge
basso	low
bivacco	bivouac hut, unmanned
bosco	wood
burrone	ravine
bus, busa	cirque
cabinovia	gondola car lift
caduta sassi	rock falls
campanile	rock spire (bell tower)

Italian	English
campeggio	camping, camping ground
capanna	hut
capitello	shrine
carta escursionistica	walking map
cascata	waterfall
casera	hut
caserma	barracks
castello	castle
cengia	ledge
chiuso	closed
cima	mountain peak
col	hill, mountain or saddle
corda metallica	cable (on aided route)
croce	cross
croda	steep-sided mountain
cuccetta	bunk bed
custode	hut guardian
destra	right
difficile	difficult
diga	dam
discesa	descent

Italian	English
doccia fredda/calda	cold/hot shower
est	east
facile	easy
fermata dell'autobus	bus stop
fiume	river
fontana	fountain
forcella	saddle, pass
funivia	cable-car
galleria	tunnel
gettone	token for a shower in the huts
ghiacciaio	glacier
giro	tour
grande	large
grotta	cave
lago	lake
malga	mountain farm, sometimes a refuge
meridionale	south
meteo	weather forecast
mezzo	middle
molino, mulino	mill
monte	mountain
nevaio	snow field
nord	north
nuovo percorso	new routing
occidente	west
ometto	cairn (little man)

Italian	English
orario	timetable
orientale	east
orrido	ravine
ovest	west
pala	rounded mountain
panificio	bakery
passo	saddle, pass
percorso alpinistico/attrezzato	climbing/aided route
pericolo	danger
pian	level ground
piccolo	small
ponte	bridge
previsioni del tempo	weather forecast
pronto soccorso	first aid
punta	mountain peak
ricovero	shelter
ricovero invernale	winter shelter adjoining a refuge
rifugio	manned mountain hut
rio	mountain stream
ristoro	refreshments
salita	ascent
scorciatoia	shortcut
seggiovia	chair lift
sella	saddle, pass
sentiero	path

Italian	English
sentiero alpinistico/ attrezzato	climbing/aided route
settentrionale	north
sinistra	left
soccorso alpino	mountain rescue
sorgente	spring (water)
spiz	mountain peak
stazione ferroviaria	railway station
strada	road
sud	south
tabià	haymaking chalet

Italian	English
tappa	route stage
telecabina	gondola car lift
teleferica	aerial cableway
torre	tower
torrente	mountain stream
val, valle, vallone	valley
vetta	mountain peak·
via ferrata	aided climbing route
via normale	normal ascent route for climbers
vietato!	forbidden!

NOTES

DOWNLOAD THE GPX FILES

The 13 stages of Alta Via 2 are available for download from:

www.cicerone.co.uk/1097/GPX

as standard format GPX files. You should be able to load them into most online GPX systems and mobile devices, whether GPS or smartphone. You may need to convert the file into your preferred format using a conversion programme such as gpsvisualizer.com or one of the many other such websites and programmes.

When you follow this link, you will be asked for your email address and where you purchased the guidebook, and have the option to subscribe to the Cicerone e-newsletter.

www.cicerone.co.uk

LISTING OF CICERONE GUIDES

BRITISH ISLES CHALLENGES, COLLECTIONS AND ACTIVITIES

Cycling Land's End to John o' Groats
Great Walks on the England Coast Path
The Big Rounds
The Book of the Bivvy
The Book of the Bothy
The Mountains of England & Wales:
  Vol 1 Wales
  Vol 2 England
The National Trails
Walking the End to End Trail

SHORT WALKS SERIES

Short Walks Hadrian's Wall
Short Walks in Arnside and Silverdale
Short Walks in Dumfries and Galloway
Short Walks in Nidderdale
Short Walks in the Lake District: Windermere Ambleside and Grasmere
Short Walks in the Surrey Hills
Short Walks Lake District – Coniston and Langdale
Short Walks on the Malvern Hills
Short Walks Winchester

SCOTLAND

Ben Nevis and Glen Coe
Cycle Touring in Northern Scotland
Cycling in the Hebrides
Cycling the North Coast 500
Great Mountain Days in Scotland
Mountain Biking in Southern and Central Scotland
Mountain Biking in West and North West Scotland
Not the West Highland Way Scotland
Scotland's Best Small Mountains
Scotland's Mountain Ridges
Scottish Wild Country Backpacking
Skye's Cuillin Ridge Traverse
The Borders Abbeys Way
The Great Glen Way
The Great Glen Way Map Booklet
The Hebridean Way
The Hebrides
The Isle of Mull
The Isle of Skye
The Skye Trail
The Southern Upland Way
The West Highland Way
The West Highland Way Map Booklet
Walking Ben Lawers, Rannoch and Atholl
Walking in the Cairngorms

Walking in the Pentland Hills
Walking in the Scottish Borders
Walking in the Southern Uplands
Walking in Torridon, Fisherfield, Fannichs and An Teallach
Walking Loch Lomond and the Trossachs
Walking on Arran
Walking on Harris and Lewis
Walking on Jura, Islay and Colonsay
Walking on Rum and the Small Isles
Walking on the Orkney and Shetland Isles
Walking on Uist and Barra
Walking the Cape Wrath Trail
Walking the Corbetts
  Vol 1 South of the Great Glen
  Vol 2 North of the Great Glen
Walking the Galloway Hills
Walking the John o' Groats Trail
Walking the Munros
  Vol 1 – Southern, Central and Western Highlands
  Vol 2 – Northern Highlands and the Cairngorms
Winter Climbs in the Cairngorms
Winter Climbs: Ben Nevis and Glen Coe

NORTHERN ENGLAND ROUTES

Cycling the Reivers Route
Cycling the Way of the Roses
Hadrian's Cycleway
Hadrian's Wall Path
Hadrian's Wall Path Map Booklet
The Coast to Coast Cycle Route
The Coast to Coast Walk
The Coast to Coast Walk Map Booklet
The Pennine Way
The Pennine Way Map Booklet
Walking the Dales Way
Walking the Dales Way Map Booklet

NORTH-EAST ENGLAND, YORKSHIRE DALES AND PENNINES

Cycling in the Yorkshire Dales
Great Mountain Days in the Pennines
Mountain Biking in the Yorkshire Dales
The Cleveland Way and the Yorkshire Wolds Way
The Cleveland Way Map Booklet
The North York Moors
Trail and Fell Running in the Yorkshire Dales
Walking in County Durham
Walking in Northumberland
Walking in the North Pennines

Walking in the Yorkshire Dales: North and East
Walking in the Yorkshire Dales: South and West
Walking St Cuthbert's Way
Walking St Oswald's Way and Northumberland Coast Path

NORTH-WEST ENGLAND AND THE ISLE OF MAN

Cycling the Pennine Bridleway
Isle of Man Coastal Path
The Lancashire Cycleway
The Lune Valley and Howgills
Walking in Cumbria's Eden Valley
Walking in Lancashire
Walking in the Forest of Bowland and Pendle
Walking on the Isle of Man
Walking on the West Pennine Moors
Walking the Ribble Way
Walks in Silverdale and Arnside

LAKE DISTRICT

Bikepacking in the Lake District
Cycling in the Lake District
Great Mountain Days in the Lake District
Joss Naylor's Lakes, Meres and Waters of the Lake District
Lake District Winter Climbs
Lake District: High Level and Fell Walks
Lake District: Low Level and Lake Walks
Mountain Biking in the Lake District
Outdoor Adventures with Children – Lake District
Scrambles in the Lake District – North
Scrambles in the Lake District – South
Trail and Fell Running in the Lake District
Walking The Cumbria Way
Walking the Lake District Fells:
  Borrowdale
  Buttermere
  Coniston
  Keswick
  Langdale
  Mardale and the Far East
  Patterdale
  Wasdale
Walking the Tour of the Lake District

DERBYSHIRE, PEAK DISTRICT AND MIDLANDS

Cycling in the Peak District
Dark Peak Walks
Scrambles in the Dark Peak
Walking in Derbyshire

CICERONE

Trust Cicerone to guide your next adventure,
wherever it may be around the world...

Discover guides for hiking, mountain walking, backpacking,
trekking, trail running, cycling and mountain biking, ski touring,
climbing and scrambling in Britain, Europe and worldwide.

Connect with Cicerone online and find inspiration.

- buy books and ebooks
- articles, advice and trip reports
- podcasts and live events
- GPX files and updates
- regular newsletter

cicerone.co.uk

The south face of the Marmolada can be admired en route to Forca Rossa (Stage 6)

ALTA VIA 2 – TREKKING IN
THE DOLOMITES

With some steep and exposed sections, the Alta Via 2 is a challenging but highly rewarding trek through Italy's magnificent Dolomites, one of six Alta Via routes that traverse the range. The 174km hut-to-hut trail from Bressanone (Brixen) to Feltre celebrates the region's spectacular scenery, visiting the Plose massif, the jagged Puez-Odle, fortress-like Sella, the majestic Marmolada (the highest mountain in the Dolomites at 3342m), Pale di San Martino and the Alpi Feltrine group.

This map booklet of Kompass 1:25,000 maps is part of a two-volume guide to this classic trek. It contains the full and up-to-date route of the trail, showing stages and variants.

The accompanying guidebook *Alta Via 2 – Trekking in the Dolomites* describes the route in 13 stages from north to south and includes comprehensive notes on accommodation, advice on transport and equipment, and a wealth of information about the region's rich geology, plants and wildlife. Also included in the guide are brief outlines of Alte Vie 3–6, which are more demanding and involve sections of via ferrata.

© Cicerone Press 2022
Reprinted 2024
ISBN: 978 1 78631 099 6

All photographs are by the author unless otherwise stated

Printed in China on responsibly sourced paper on behalf of
Latitude Press Ltd

© KOMPASSKarten GmbH cartography
licence number: 41-0921-LIV

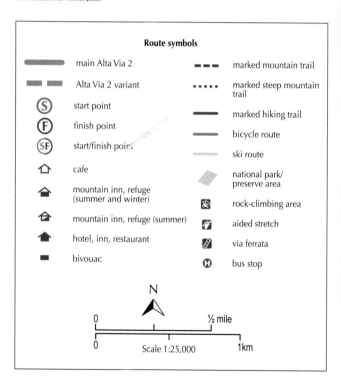

Route symbols

main Alta Via 2		marked mountain trail	
Alta Via 2 variant		marked steep mountain trail	
(S) start point		marked hiking trail	
(F) finish point		bicycle route	
(SF) start/finish point		ski route	
cafe		national park/preserve area	
mountain inn, refuge (summer and winter)		rock-climbing area	
mountain inn, refuge (summer)		aided stretch	
hotel, inn, restaurant		via ferrata	
bivouac		(H) bus stop	

N

0 ——— ½ mile

0 ——— 1km

Scale 1:25,000

ALTA VIA 2 – TREKKING IN THE DOLOMITES

Stage maps

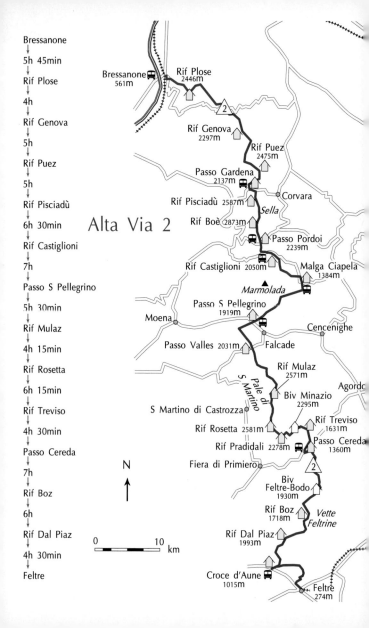

Alta Via 2

Bressanone
561m

Rif Plose
2446m

Rif Genova
2297m

Rif Puez
2475m

Passo Gardena
2137m

Corvara

Rif Pisciadù 2587m

Sella

Rif Boè 2873m

Passo Pordoi
2239m

Rif Castiglioni 2050m

Malga Ciapela
1384m

Marmolada

Passo S Pellegrino
1919m

Moena

Cencenighe

Passo Valles 2031m

Falcade

Rif Mulaz
2571m

Agordo

Biv Minazio
2295m

Pale di S Martino

S Martino di Castrozza

Rif Treviso
1631m

Rif Rosetta 2581m

Rif Pradidali 2278m

Passo Cereda
1360m

Fiera di Primiero

Biv Feltre-Bodo
1930m

Rif Boz
1718m

Vette Feltrine

Rif Dal Piaz
1993m

Croce d'Aune
1015m

Feltre
274m

N

0   10 km

ROUTE SUMMARY TABLE – NORTH TO SOUTH

Stage no.	Start	Finish	Distance	Time	Ascent	Descent	Grade	Page no.
1	Bressanone	Rifugio Plose	12km	5hr 45min	1910m	20m	2	6
2	Rifugio Plose	Rifugio Genova	13.5km	4hr	680m	530m	2	8
3	Rifugio Genova	Rifugio Puez	12km	5hr	840m	660m	2–3	12
4	Rifugio Puez	Rifugio Pisciadù	10km	5hr	900m	800m	3	14
5	Rifugio Pisciadù	Rifugio Castiglioni	16km	6hr 30min	690m	1230m	3	17
6	Rifugio Castiglioni	Passo San Pellegrino	22km	7hr	1110m	1240m	2	21
7	Passo San Pellegrino	Rifugio Mulaz	13km	5hr 30min	1040m	380m	3	26
8	Rifugio Mulaz	Rifugio Rosetta	7.5km	4hr 15min	750m	740m	3+	30
9	Rifugio Rosetta	Rifugio Treviso	13km	6hr 15min	790m	1740m	3	32
10	Rifugio Treviso	Passo Cereda	8.5km	4hr 30min	750m	1010m	2–3	34
11	Passo Cereda	Rifugio Boz	13.5km	7hr	1250m	900m	3	36
12	Rifugio Boz	Rifugio Dal Piaz	14km	6hr	940m	670m	3	39
13	Rifugio Dal Piaz	Feltre	19km	4hr 30min	neglible	1820m	2	43
Total	Bressanone	Feltre	174km	71hr 15min	11,650m	11,740m		

Krone

Forum Brixen

Diözesan-Museum

Krakofl

Grüner Baum

Ober-kamol

6

BRIXEN
BRESSANONE

561

Karlspromenade

Unterkar

930
Moardorf
Villa

Mistrol

Mission
Comboni

Millanderhof

Milland

Millan

Maria
im Sand

4A

Trametschbach

12A

Mellaun
Meluno

Gasser-hof

Bachgut

Ratzöt

Eisack
F. Isarco

Pallaus

Kampan

Stage 1	
Start	Bressanone
Distance	12km
Time	5hr 45min
Ascent	1910m
Descent	20m
Grade	2

Klerant
Cleran

Frötscher

Unter-
Plattner

18

St. Andrä
Rundweg

Bar Sams

Sarns
Sarnes

Rumml

Fischer

Oberplanetz

Planser

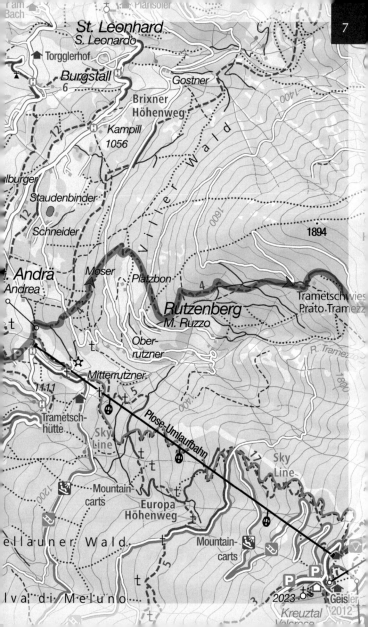

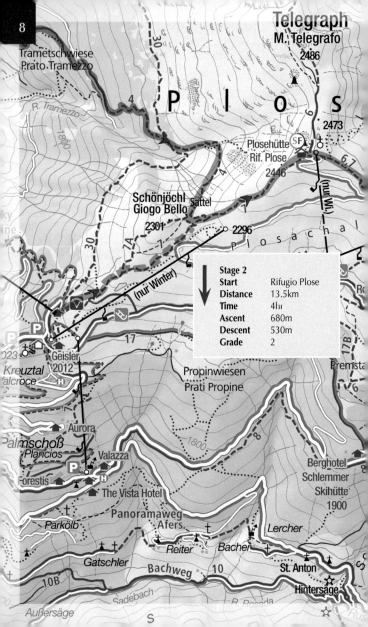

Telegraph
M. Telegrafo
2486

Trametschwiese
Prato Tramezzo

R. Tramezzo

P l o s

2473

Plosehütte
Rif. Plose
2446

Schönjöchl
Giogo Bello
2301

Sattel

2296

Plosachal

(nur Wi.)

(nur Winter)

Stage 2
Start   Rifugio Plose
Distance   13.5km
Time   4lı
Ascent   680m
Descent   530m
Grade   2

Kreuztal
alcroce

Geisler
2012

Propinwiesen
Prati Propine

17

17B

Premsta

Aurora

Palmschoß
Plancios

Valazza

Forestis

The Vista Hotel

Berghotel
Schlemmer
Skihütte
1900

Panoramaweg
Afers

Parkölb

Reiter

Bacher

Lercher

Gatschler

Bachweg   10

St. Anton

Hintersäge

Außersäge

Sadebach

R. Posada

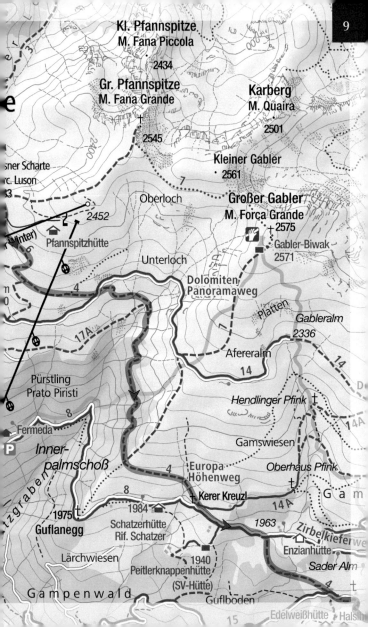

Kl. Pfannspitze
M. Fana Piccola
2434

Gr. Pfannspitze
M. Fana Grande
† 2545

Karberg
M. Quaira
2501

Kleiner Gabler
• 2561

Oberloch

Großer Gabler
M. Forca Grande
† 2575

Gabler-Biwak
2571

Pfannspitzhütte

Unterloch

Dolomiten
Panoramaweg

Platten

Gableralm
2336

2452

sner Scharte
rc. Luson
3

(Inter)

17A

Afereralm

14

Pürstling
Prato Piristi

Hendlinger Pfink †

Fermeda

P

8

Gamswiesen

Inner-
palmschoß

4

Europa
Höhenweg

Oberhaus Pfink †

Gam

† 1975

Guflanegg

Lärchwiesen

8

1984

Schatzerhütte
Rif. Schatzer

† Kerer Kreuzl

1963

14A

Zirbelkiefe

Enzianhütte

Sader Alm

1940
Peitlerknappenhütte
(SV-Hütte)

Guflboden

4 †

G a m p e n w a l d

tzgraben

Edelweißhütte Halslin

Stage 3	
Start	Rifugio Genova
Distance	12km
Time	5hr
Ascent	840m
Descent	660m
Grade	2–3

Naturpark Puez-Geisler · Parc Naturel Puez-Odle

Dolora

4B

4

Cianc

Munt dla Crusc 2300

Forcela de Pütia
Peitlerscharte
2357

4B

Europa
Höhenw

TMV

2340

Kreuzkofeljoch
Pso Poma

Ju dla Crusc

Bronsürch

Gunther
Messner-Steig

Ringspitz
2625

Wörndle Lochalm

Zendleser Kofel
Col dl' Poma
2422

Schlüterhütte
Rif. Genova
2306 SF

3

35

Dolorama

35 35

Aferer Geisler
Odle d'Eores

Alta Via G. Messner

2599

Kaserillam
1920

31

32

37A

33

Gampenalm
2062

2646

R. Caseril

Kaserilbach

31

Gampenwiese

1975

33

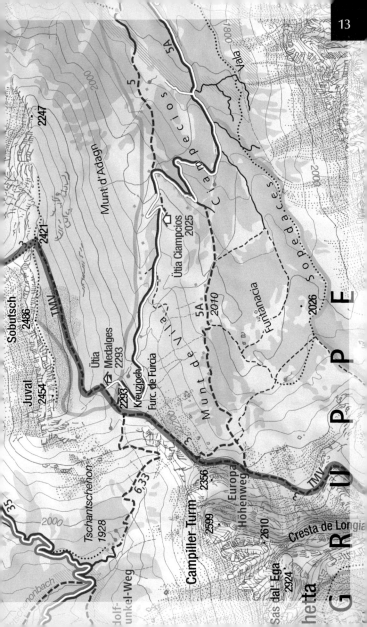

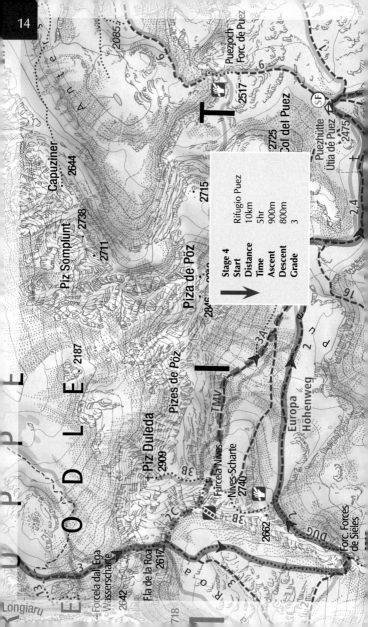

14

Puezjoch
Forc. de Puez

2085

6

2517

Puezhütte
Ütia de Puez

Col del Puez
2725

2475

2·4

Stage 4	
Start	Rifugio Puez
Distance	10km
Time	5hr
Ascent	900m
Descent	800m
Grade	3

Piza de Pöz

2715

2187

Piz Somplunt
2711
2738
2644

Capuziner

Pizes de Pöz

Piz Duleda
2909

TMV

3B

3A

Forcela Nives
Nives-Scharte
2740

2662

Europa
Höhenweg

DUG

Forc. Forces
de Sieles

Forcela dal Ega
Wasserscharte
2642

Fla de la Roa
2617

3

Longiaru

718

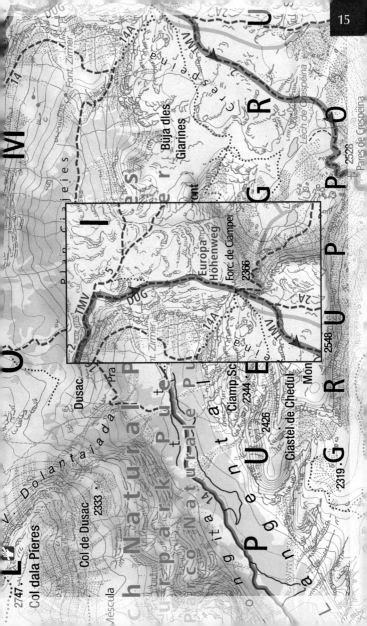

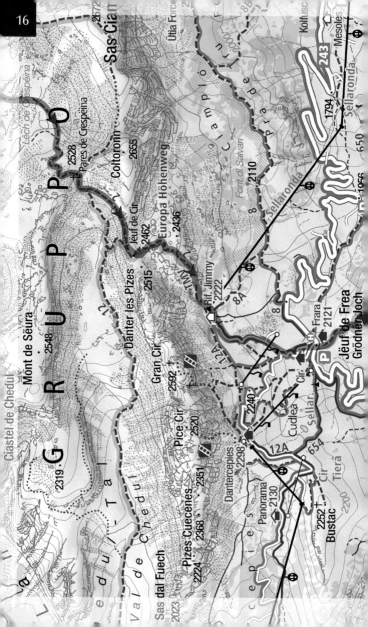

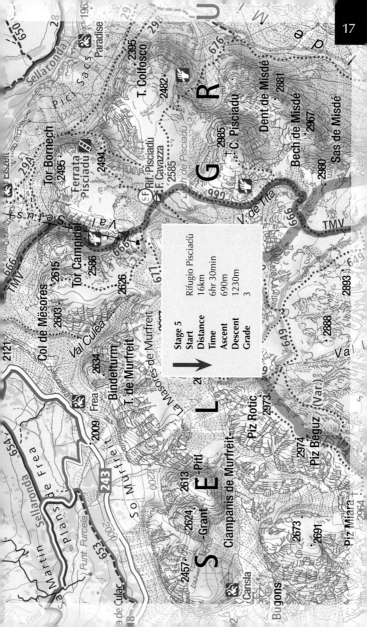

Stage 5	
Start	Rifugio Pisciadù
Distance	16km
Time	6hr 30min
Ascent	690m
Descent	1230m
Grade	3

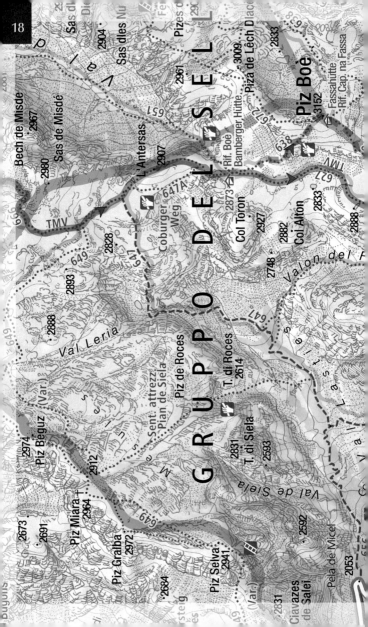

nt de Vauz
1839

Bosch de la Viza

Plan de la Carpacia

Portados
2158

S a l e r e

Sent. Geologico
Arabba

Sellaronda

680

Sellaronda

s da Ciapel
2557

2379   La Forfesc
Col de Paussa   2585

Porta
Vescovo

Viel dal Pan   Belvedere
2648

2379   DTK   Rif. L. Gorza
2478

Pre de Val   P è l e s   TMV

601   601A   Val de Fedaa

698

Pre   P è l e s   DTK

698   2238

Stage 6	
Start	Rifugio Castiglioni
Distance	22km
Time	7hr
Ascent	1110m
Descent	1240m
Grade	2

2058   SF
Rif. Castiglioni
Marmolada

Lago

TMV

Alla Diga   Vernel

Via dei
Rusci   Rif. Dolomia
2074   Cima Undici

Museo della
Grande Guerra

La Man

Ciamorciaa   619   618   Col di Bousc
2494

Ferrata
Ombretta

Sasso Vernale
3058

612

Pas de Ombretola
2864

Ombretola

612B

2931　Sforcela del Bachet
2836

Valon de Ombretta

Sas Piat
2650

Formenton
2937

2770

3009

de Jigolé
2815

Sas de Valfreida

2875
Pulpito di Fulchiade

M.la Banca

2875

P.zo le Crene
2760

Val der Meda

693　2350
2346

Forca Rossa

M.le Saline
2402

2

(Var.)

2176

670

2363

Altá Via dei Pastori
Pian de la Schita

Le Marmolade

Rif. Fuciade
1982

670

2088

P.zo Forca
2285

1974

607

DTK

670

2

(Var.)

694

Val di Forca

631

M.ga Bosch
Brusa
1867

Casoni
di Valfredda

1908

Sass de
la Palaza
2214

691

2171

Pale del Fop
2050

V. del Fop

Fop
2892

Tere Ross

689

684

M. C
21

(Var.) △2

Franzedàz

Forzèla

...la del Om

Val de Franzedàz

L'A

2313

Cime dell'Auta

Ferrata
Paolin-Piccolin

Occidentale

Forc. di
Medil

2624

2622

Orientale

2602

Barbagin
2524

Sassedel
2337

689

2312
Psn del Col Becher

2444
Col Becher

Alta Via dei Pastori

Acqua di Foch

Ric: Baita Papa
Giovanni Paolo I

1865

696

689

Le Fontane

Alta Via dei Pas

Le Fraide

Baita dei
Cacciatori
1751

1675

2060

689

Ciamp

pian de le Fratte

M. Vallesella
2020

692

Valle Tegosse

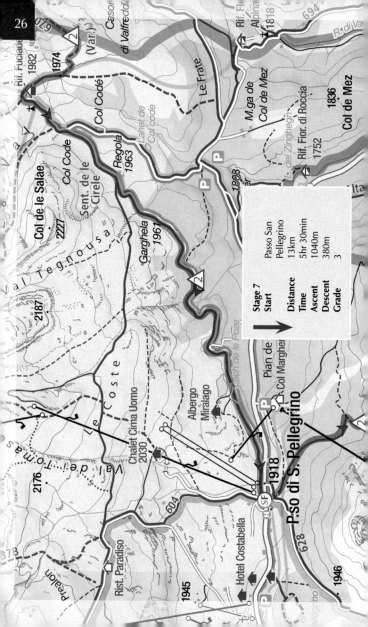

Stage 7
Start Passo San Pellegrino

Distance 13km
Time 5hr 30min
Ascent 1040m
Descent 380m
Grade 3

28

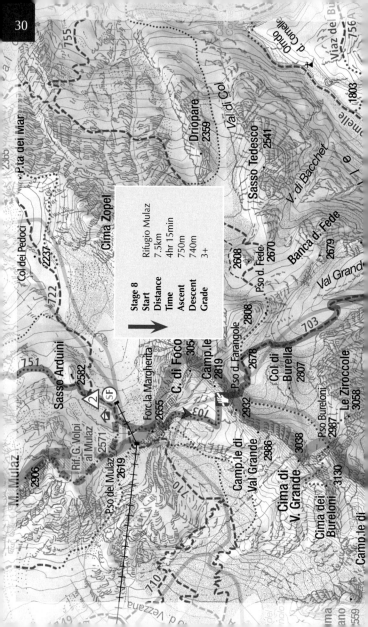

Stage 8	
Start	Rifugio Mulaz
Distance	7.5km
Time	4hr 15min
Ascent	750m
Descent	740m
Grade	3+

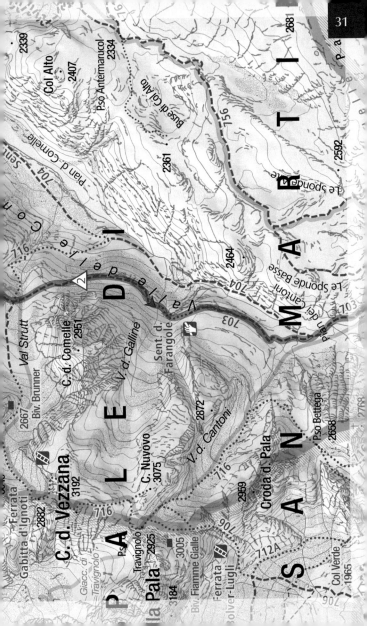

Map continues on page 35

Pala Cri

2090

Cam.le d'Ostia

2405

V.ne Sedole

Sent. d. Sedole

Portela

M.ga Pradidali (rud.)

1428

Pra d'Ostio

B.ta Don Bosco

1231

709

Madonna della Neve

P.so d. Fradusta

2670

709A

Fratte

1338

709

709

709

V. Pradidali

719

Troi de Rodena

Pedemonte

1592

719

Prad

Le Sponde Basse

Prau dei Cantoni

703

757

756

703

707

703

Cima d. Scarpe

2802

·2788

M A

N

Pso Bettega

2658

†2768

C. Corona

701

2581

Rif. Rosetta G: Pedrotti

SF

Pso di Rosetta

2572

701A

Pso di Val di Roda

2572

·2694

Rodetta

Croda di Roda

Col d. Fede

2278

2

C. Rosetta

2743

da d. Pala

701

702

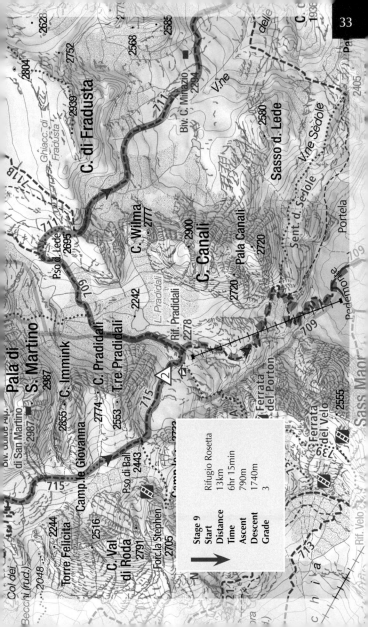

Stage 9	
Start	Rifugio Rosetta
Distance	13km
Time	6hr 15min
Ascent	790m
Descent	1740m
Grade	3

Stage 10	
Start	Rifugio Treviso
Distance	8.5km
Time	4hr 30min
Ascent	750m
Descent	1010m
Grade	2-3

Com. Sagron-Mi

Stage 11	
Start	Passo Cereda
Distance	13.5km
Time	7hr
Ascent	1250m
Descent	900m
Grade	3

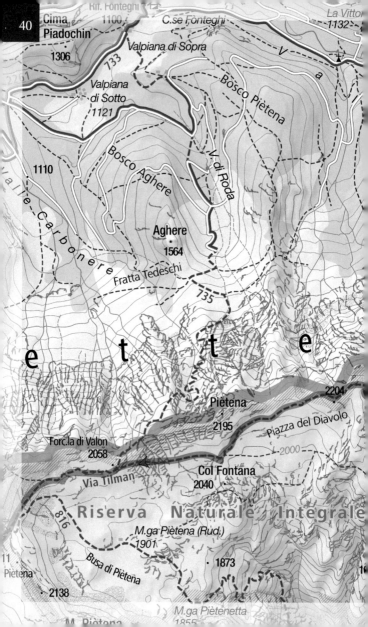

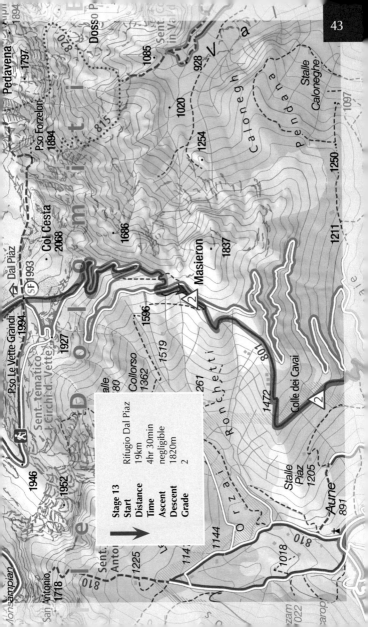

Stage 13
Start Rifugio Dal Piaz
Distance 19km
Time 4hr 30min
Ascent negligible
Descent 1820m
Grade 2

Stalle alla
Fornace 743

V. So

1008

M. Pafagài †
1047

Crocera
728

Sent. Chiesette
pedemontane

Agritur.
Val di Lamen

970

t. Chiesette
montane

Maragno

Paradiso

La Fastreda

Il Capitello
730

Salenza

Pra Mauro
685

527
Sorg.
del Toro

Costa

Saluc

Lame
568

Salzena

Monegat

L
a
m
e

V.la Elisa
585

466

702

Valduna

Case
Pascoli

Nòrcen
489

Carpene

435

Colonia
S. Marco

Tratt.
Alpina

Convento

Casanova

415

2

C.tro Visitatori
Parco Dolomiti
Bellunesi

Murle
344

Altor

Il Sasso
nello Stagno

Pedavena
359

i

Villa
Berton

Foèn
313

La Casazza

348

V.la

321

442

S. Anna

Starnui

377

Rio Ligont

Pasquer

Villa
Binotto

B.go Ruga

Museo
Civico

FELTRE
325

Colle del Laro

Colle alle Coste
319

S. Fermo

CICERONE

Trust Cicerone to guide your next adventure, wherever it may be around the world...

Discover guides for hiking, mountain walking, backpacking, trekking, trail running, cycling and mountain biking, ski touring, climbing and scrambling in Britain, Europe and worldwide.

Connect with Cicerone online and find inspiration.

- buy books and ebooks
- articles, advice and trip reports
- podcasts and live events
- GPX files and updates
- regular newsletter

cicerone.co.uk